Black Boys Can Make It
How they overcome the obstacles to university in the UK and USA

Black Boys Can Make It
How they overcome the obstacles to university in the UK and USA

Cheron Byfield

Foreword by Lord Herman Ouseley

Trentham Books

Stoke on Trent, UK and Sterling, USA

Trentham Books Limited

Westview House   22883 Quicksilver Drive
734 London Road   Sterling
Oakhill   VA 20166-2012
Stoke on Trent   USA
Staffordshire
England ST4 5NP

First published 2008

British Library Cataloguing-in-Publication Data
A catalogue record for this book is available from the British Library

ISBN: 978 1 85856 431 9

Designed and typeset by Trentham Print Design Ltd, Chester and printed in Great Britain by Cromwell Press Ltd, Trowbridge.

Contents

Dedication

*This book is dedicated to my nephew, Michael Taylor,
my godsons, Simon Oliver and Jakim Gregory,
and all the boys who are on, or who have been on a
Black Boys Can project*

*All royalties from this book are donated to the
Black Boys Can project*

Acknowledgements

I wish to acknowledge Professor Geoffrey Walford, my former supervisor from the University of Oxford, and also Professor Sally Tomlinson for their guidance and support throughout the years I undertook the empirical research in preparation for this book. I am also indebted to Trentham Books, particularly Dr Gillian Klein for her constructive criticisms of my earlier drafts.

I also wish to acknowledge all the students from the universities of Oxford, Wolverhampton, Central Florida and Harvard, who took part in this study. Without their willingness to give up their valued time, this study could not have been conducted.

I must commend my beautiful nieces: Cerise, Crystal, Nicole and Paris, for achieving so well at school. Although the focus of my book in not on girls, but there is much they can glean to help them on their journey from school to higher education. I particularly wish to thank my parents Vincent and Vira and also my sisters, Audrey and Annette, for their moral support throughout the period of my research.

In loving memory of my late Pastor, Elder, C. L. Gregory, his grandson Lawrence is featured on the front cover of this book. Elder Gregory provided me with so much moral support in my own pursuit of higher education. Lawrence, who made it into university, was also amongst the first cohort of boys to join the Black Boys Can project in 1999.

Above all, I must acknowledge my Lord and Saviour Jesus Christ for giving me the strength to overcome all the major challenges I faced in the process of undertaking the empirical research in preparation for writing this book.

Foreword

When Black youths read about themselves, it goes something like this: you are a persistently under-performing group; you are six times more likely to be excluded from school and be a young offender; you may already be in a gang or likely to join one. The likely causes of your condition are: absentee fathers; absence of positive male role models; and being surrounded by women who cannot control or motivate you. You aim too low and do not believe people like you can succeed. Yet the reality is that there are a large number of young black males with high aspirations, who have a focus on learning and who succeed. Often, these young men come from the same background as those who are under-achieving at school, or involved with the criminal justice system. It is a sad fact that we seldom hear about these young people. (Professor Gus John, *The Guardian*, 25 August 2008)

For more than four decades, educationists, community activists, politicians, Black parents, the media and social commentators have expressed serious concerns about the educational underachievement of Black boys. Many of the actions to tackle this phenomenon have been generated in the Black community itself, with the establishment of Supplementary Schools, learning programmes and campaigns against biased teaching in the classroom that especially affect all the children from deprived backgrounds. Deep concern about under-achievement persists, despite some measurable progress being made. Community-led initiatives have been major contributors to such successes. Dynamic Black leaders have been scathing in their criticism of the government for failing to engage with local Black male achievers and instead imposing its own top-down programmes which have tended to result in failure.

John champions the qualities of the majority of Black males, who have 'a highly developed sense of social justice, an abhorrence of oppression, a determination to affirm and safeguard their own rights and entitlements, have high aspirations and self-management skills'. Others including Diane Abbott MP, Tony Sewell, Maud Blair, Cecile Wright, Trevor Phillips, Ansel Wong and Professor Chris Mullard have similarly challenged the institutional failures of the education establishment to end underachievement and are stressing the factors which work to produce better outcomes for Black boys.

Now we can welcome this contribution by Cheron Byfield. *Black Boys Can Make It* highlights the factors that contribute to Black boys from deprived backgrounds achieving higher education success. Her study of 40 Black students at universities in the USA and the UK provides confirmation of much of what is already known by the Black community activists in the UK who are exemplars of the positive male role models who remain 'invisible' to the political and decision-making system in public institutions and thus excluded from being part of the solution to the problem of underachievement.

Byfield's study shows that Black boys can and do succeed, in spite of a system that is loaded in favour of the haves as opposed to the have-nots, biased in favour of one class of individuals against another and favourable towards one race against another. Even though they experience the same deprived backgrounds as the boys who underachieve, with absentee fathers, inadequate housing, teachers' low expectations of them, peer group pressure to reject education as 'uncool', racism and stereotyped negative identities, these boys can and do succeed.

Their success can be put down to a combination of personal ambition, parental support, empathetic teaching, willingness to learn, self-belief and self confidence, commitment to hard work, acknowledgment of the value and benefits of educational achievements, a determination to work their way out of poverty, developing a competitive nature and life-style, not allowing distractions or disparagement even from friends and peer groups to deter them from achieving their personal goals and, above all, taking personal responsibility for organising their lives and not looking to blame others for any of their shortcomings, failures, disappointments and setbacks.

My own life-long experiences of ascending out of dire poverty, squalor, and deprivation were most influenced and driven by the fierce determination shown by my mother that her children must work hard and stand on their own two feet to succeed and work their way out of poverty. The process was to grab every opportunity going, take any help offered, make the most of any good fortune or luck coming our way and strive to become self reliant as soon as possible. With such a mother as a role model you don't look for an absentee father. You are kept busy and not idle, you absorb the work ethic and you admire the graft and commitment of immigrants taking on two, three, or four jobs at a time to make ends meet and to support their families. Most important for me was accepting responsibility for all my personal actions and calling upon the inculcated mantra of: 'if you do not succeed as planned, try again, try again' ever more determinedly and keeping on trying creatively and in different ways, notwithstanding the frustrations caused by repeated rejection.

The challenge for our society in fulfilling our obligations to current and future generations of children is that of making each child feel special as a person and believe in themselves, whatever their backgrounds, circumstances or appearances. There is a realisation on the part of the British government that this is a challenge to be met through its Every Child Matters agenda. However, this is not reflected in outcomes and not every child is enabled to feel special and to believe that they are blessed with ability and have opportunities to be supported and assisted to succeed. Their earliest years are very influential in their development and their conditioning, background, circumstances and positive learning opportunities will, more often than not, set them on a path towards either a successful or a blighted future.

At a time in the UK when concerns about knife and gun crime among young people are concentrating the minds of the public at large and the directly affected local communities in particular, the government should be leading, taking forward the agenda to end educational underachievement, especially by meaningly involving those who have been there and done it.

One member of government who has been there and is doing it is David Lammy MP, the most senior black person currently in the government, a graduate of Harvard. He represents residents in one of the most deprived parts of the London Borough of Haringey and is a Minister in the Department of Innovation, Universities and Skills. Recently, in The New Statesman, he has commented on these issues, warning of a 'dearth of male role models, alienation and under-performance of boys' and pointing to the 'fetishisation of money and the growth of consumerism as creating new pressures' for young people. He asserted that such pressures were contributing to a 'get rich or die quick' culture among the young men now engaged in knife and gun related crimes instead of focusing their efforts on the acquisition of educational attainment and skills. What he failed to say was how much his own government's policies have fuelled the fetish for style rather than substance, for 'bling', celebrity adulation and glitz, consumerism and a get rich culture.

As chickens come home to roost in more ways than one, Cheron Byfield's book helps to concentrate the mind on what the true challenge is for us and what we have to do to enable not only Black boys to achieve educationally, but all our young people: it is they who are special and who represent the future.

Sir Herman Ouseley,
House of Lords, England, September 2008

Preface

There is a plethora of research focusing on the underachievement of Black boys but little attention has been paid to those who are academically successful. This research project sets out to investigate whether Black male students in the USA and UK who have successfully accessed higher education were exposed to the factors found to correlate with the extensively researched underachievement of these groups. I seek to identify the factors that have led to their educational success and influenced their access to and choice of universities.

The main vehicle for data collection was a qualitative interviewing research strategy. Using a stratified purposeful sampling technique, I studied a sample of 40 Black male students under the age of 25 who had been educated in the UK or the USA. The students had a diverse range of social class background, family structure and degree disciplines. To add to the diversity the study included students who attended both new and ancient universities – ten students from each – and two universities in each country.

The study found that these successful students were not immune from the factors which so often impede Black boys' success. They were subjected to racism, adverse peer pressure and, in many cases, poor social and economic circumstances. Furthermore, the study revealed that not all the students were conformist – most had displayed non-conformist behaviour at school. But they succeeded academically because they had varying degrees of compensatory factors in their lives which provided a buffer against the adverse circumstances which surrounded their schooling experiences.

Supportive parents with strong educational values, strong religious beliefs and affiliations, excellent teachers, Black and White, and access to community interventionists programmes all played a part. In addition, the students had to use certain strategies and make enormous personal sacrifices. Although Bourdieu's cultural capital theory provides a useful framework for discussing the issues, it nonetheless has limitations for a study of this nature because it fails to give due recognition to key forces in the subjects' lives: race and racism.

Although they encountered debilitating disadvantages and constraints during their school years, the boys in this study got to where they wanted. However, their success is no justification for a society in which certain students face particular challenges in their pursuit of academic success. The demands that were made of these students are over and above what any child in an affluent society should be expected to make in order to obtain a good education.

PART ONE
SETTING THE SCENE

1

Introduction

Black boys are not a homogeneous group. Contrary to popular view, they are not synonymous with underachievement. Many do achieve academically. Yet the press is littered with headlines about the underachievement of Black boys and a plethora of academic research focuses on the negative outcomes of their schooling. This persistent deficit model reinforces negative stereotypes and adversely affects their expectations, creating a self fulfilling prophecy. Little is known about Black boys who do achieve academic success. As a researcher and also a co-founder of the National Black Boys Can Association, a national educational project established to raise the attainment of Black boys throughout the UK, I was determined to redress this imbalance. This book is a tribute to all those Black boys in the UK and USA who have achieved against all odds.

Conceptualisation and definition

I make constant reference to the terms 'race', 'Black' and 'social class' and therefore define what I mean by them.

Race

The conceptualisation of the term 'race' has been heavily debated. During the nineteenth century the term was used by biologists to distinguish between groups that, they thought, shared a common biological ancestry. Assumptions were made about physical and mental differences, and these assumptions were used to justify the subordination of Black people by White people (Mason, 1986) by means of such 'scientific racism'. But it is difficult to define a rationale for racial categories and no objective set of categories has been agreed. Genetic studies have found some evidence of broad 'continental' groups which are genetically similar (Burchard *et al*, 2003), but there is little evidence that these correspond to commonly perceived racial categories (Cooper *et al*, 2003). Donald and Rattansi, (1992) assert that 'in genetic terms, the physical and biological differences between groups defined as 'races' have been shown to be trivial [and] no persuasive empirical case has been made for ascribing common psychological, intellectual or moral capacities or characteristics to individuals on the basis of skin colour or physiognomy'. Similarly, Rosenberg *et al* (2002) argue that there is wider genetic variation between individuals within one racial group (such as White) than there is between such 'racial' groups, as 93 to 95 per cent of genetic variation is within population groups.

The notion of biologically distinct human races is now discredited: as indeed there is only one race, the human race. However, the term race is still used today, not in a biological but in a social sense. The notion of 'social race' has emerged to refer to groups of people who are socially defined as sharing common characteristics. As Archer (2003) points out, 'because racism remains a powerful force within society, we still need a way to engage with racial issues and the effects of racism while simultaneously recognising that the concept of race itself is sociologically constructed and is not a natural or biological phenomenon'. The term race is used in this book within the framework of 'social race'.

Black
The concept of Black in relation to people took on political connotations with the rise of Black activism in the USA in the 1960s. The term was reclaimed as a source of pride and identity, challenging the negative connotations relating to the word, such as Blackleg and Blacklist. In the UK, the term Black began to be used during the 1960s and 1970s as a banner for all minority ethnic groups to rally beneath and politically resist and struggle against colour based racism. However, the term caused controversy because not all minority ethnic groups felt equally well represented by it (Modood, 1994). Today, Black is used in the UK for people who have a shared history of European colonialism, neo-colonialism, imperialism, ethnocentrism and racism and embraces those who experience structural and institutional discrimination because of their skin colour.

Black people had earlier been called 'Negroes', 'Coloured people' and 'West Indians'. As used today, and in this book, Black refers to people of African descent (Africans, African-Caribbeans and African Americans) and to people mixed or dual heritage, with one parent of African descent. It is also how the Office of National Statistics used it in the British 2001 Census.

Social class

Classifying a student's social class is a complex affair. Do you base it upon their father's occupation, their mother's occupation, or both? How do you classify a parent who has changed their occupation or is unemployed, and how far back to you go in their employment history? Do you subscribe to Erick Olin Wright's structural Marxism (1980) or John Goldthorpe's occupational class schema (1982) or others? Questions abound.

I came to the conclusion that none of this was appropriate for my study, because it was inappropriate to ask students detailed and sensitive questions about, for instance, their parents' income, in order to determine this. I therefore classified the students according to their parents' education qualification and occupation. However, a notable difference between the UK and the USA students is that the USA students used three classifications – working-class, lower middle-class and upper middle-class – whereas the UK students used only two – middle-class and working-class. Here I use 'lower-class' to refer to working-class students from the UK and USA as well as most of the lower middle-class American students, and 'middle-class' to refer to the middle-class students from the UK, the upper middle-class from the USA and the lower middle-class students from the USA who resembled the UK's middle-class category.

Methodology
Research questions

My study set out to answer the following questions:

1. Have Black boys in the USA and the UK who have successfully accessed higher education been exposed to the factors identified in recent literature as correlating with Black boys' underachievement?

2. What factors have contributed to the educational success of Black boys in the USA and the UK at the end of compulsory schooling?

3. What influences successful young Black males' access to and choice of universities in the UK and the USA?

Research strategy

Because so little has been written about successful Black boys' educational experiences, a qualitative study is appropriate, as it yields depth in the data rather than surface patterns. I sought a diverse range of Black male participants from the higher education institutions: participants from both the UK and the USA who had different socio-economic backgrounds, different family structures and who were studying different types of degrees.

For this exploratory study I aimed for a sample size of 40 who met the following criteria:

- They had to be under the age of 25. This was important because the study sought to reflect on the educational experiences of its respondents from primary school age upwards and I believed that their fairly recent memory of their educational experiences was likely to be more vivid from younger rather than older students'. And because the educational systems in both countries constantly change I wanted to explore the experiences of those educated in recent systems. Furthermore, the experiences of those under the age of 25 are likely to be nearer to the experiences of boys currently at school, so will be easier for them to identify with and learn from.

- They had to have had full exposure to the educational system in the UK or USA, so they only qualified for participation in the study if they had begun their education in one or other country from the age of 5.

I employed a stratified purposeful sampling technique and included a diverse range of students from the UK and the USA. Despite different educational traditions and historical experiences, Black people in these countries have much in common: most of their ancestors were subjected to slavery, they remain minorities in White dominated societies, their males are adversely positioned in social indicators such as crime and unemployment, they underachieve in schools and are under-represented in higher education. I included an equal number of students from each country.

To ensure optimal diversity among the participants, I selected a new and an ancient university in each country. Ancient universities tend to be more highly academically selective and they generally attract students from middle-class backgrounds with traditional family structures and focus on non-vocational degrees. Black students have traditionally been, severely under-represented in ancient universities and still are. The newer universities tend to be less academically selective and attract non-traditional students wishing to study more vocational orientated degrees. Many have a good or even disproportionately high representation of Black students. By focusing the study on the most extreme types of universities I was able to gather data from students with a wide variety of experiences which had contributed to their success.

The new university selected in the UK was Wolverhampton, established in 1992 when its status changed from a polytechnic. It is the fifth largest University in England and in 2006 had a comparatively large Black British student population of 8 per cent. I coupled this with the 800 year old University of Oxford, the oldest university in the English-speaking world, which prides itself in selecting 'the brightest and the best' students.

In the USA, the new university was Central Florida, established in 1963. It is now one of the largest universities in the USA with over 43,000 students. Eight per cent are Black, a minority of them male. The ancient university selected is Harvard, the oldest in the USA, established in 1636. In 2006, more than 18,000 degree students were enrolled, of whom approximately 6000 are undergraduates. Like the University of Central Florida and Wolverhampton, 8 per cent of its student population are Black. Two thirds come from public schools and about two thirds receive some form of public aid.

Interviewing

Qualitative interviewing' is used differently by and within different social science disciplines. In this study, it describes in-depth, semi-structured interviewing. As the interviews about the lives of participants were quite long, they resembled those used in life history research.

Qualitative face-to-face interviews, with pre-specified question areas, provide focus and structure whilst allowing flexibility and scope to probe beneath the surface of the responses. I was able to respond to new leads and pick up on non-verbal cues. This approach garnered rich and highly illuminating data and proved to be a powerful way to understand the students. Life history research recognises that 'lives are not hermetically compartmentalised and that consequently, anything which happens to us in one area of our lives potentially impacts upon and has implications for other areas too' (Goodson and Sikes, 2001).

Like any method of data collection however, qualitative interviewing is not free of problems. There are artefacts intrinsic to qualitative research methods, including interviews, that affect the reliability and validity of the data produced. Like any self-report method, the interview approach relies upon respondents being able and willing to give accurate and complete answers to the questions. There is always the danger that interviewees might lie. They might wish to sabotage the research, or they might dislike the interviewer, be too embarrassed to tell the truth or simply not remember the details accurately. It is impossible in this research to complement the interviews with other documents.

Another limitation is that data generated can be difficult to analyse and compare. And, like any method where the researcher is an overt participant in the data collection process, interviewing involves researcher effects. In any interview, the characteristics of the researcher – for example: demeanour, accent, dress, gender, age or race – may influence the respondents' willingness to participate and to answer accurately. But since people engage in more self-disclosure to an interviewer they find similar to themselves (Robson, 1993), the fact that I am from the same ethnic group as those I interviewed was considered to be advantageous.

The interview framework I used to help me answer the research questions was made up of closed and open-ended questions (see appendix 1).

Ethical considerations

A number of ethical guidelines have been published to, amongst other things, assist researchers in their endeavours to be ethical, including that provided by the British Educational Research Association (2003). Two main ethical considerations concerned me: informed consent and confidentiality. I sought informed consent from everyone who took part in the study. To maintain the anonymity of the students, pseudonyms will be used.

Most of the pseudonyms used here are names of men involved in the Black Boys Can Network, and most of the rest are borrowed from members of my family or my Godsons.

Data analysis

I began the research design with a conceptual framework that came to loosely mirror the interview framework, thus providing a shell for data collation. So the main areas to be studied were made apparent from the outset.

The data generated for all the research questions were analysed by countries and by university sites. I also analysed and compared the data to identify similarities and differences amongst the students. I examined the influence of external economic and social factors such as social class, their degree of exposure to adverse school experiences such as peer pressure and racism, the influences of others outside the school environment such as the family and the community, and the personal attitudes and qualities of the participants in the sample.

Themes and emerging themes

Not everyone enters the education market with equal amounts of cultural capital. I therefore introduced three categories of students in this book, the Sprinter Boys, the Relay Boys and the Marathon Boys, according to a key aspect of their cultural capital: their educational cultural heritage as it relates to their family history of participation in higher education. The main characteristics of each category are summarised in the chart below.

Sprinter Boys	Relay Boys	Marathon Boys
Boys with a family history of participation in higher education. At least one parent accessed higher education before their son entered school.	Boys whose parents accessed higher education as mature students during the latter part of their son's schooling.	Boys who are the first generation in their families to attend university.
Typically, although not always, these boys are from upper middleclass backgrounds.	Typically, although not always, these boys were from lower class backgrounds but their parents were beginning to move up the social mobility ladder.	All these boys, with the exception of one, were from lower social class backgrounds.
The strong educational background of their parents gave these boys an advantage over the Relay and Marathon boys as it endowed them with the greatest amount of cultural capital. Their parents were in a position to nurture them with distinctive cultural tastes, knowledge, abilities, habits, attitudes and beliefs, thus making them better equipped to pursue higher education. And being in the most educationally advantageous position they had a shorter race to run in pursuit of higher education than either the Relay or Marathon Boys	Their parents began to gain more cultural capital as they re-entered the educational system as mature students. This increased cultural capital placed these parents in a position to equip their sons with the dispositions of manner and thought to help them progress into higher education. However, this process is likely to have started late in their sons schooling, and hence these boys had a longer run to race than the Sprinter Boys, but they did have a parent who could 'pass them the baton'.	Their parents had the least amount of cultural capital. Through cultural reproduction, existing disadvantages and inequalities are passed down from one generation to the next. These boys were in the most education disadvantaged position, and therefore at high risk of being eliminated from access to higher education. They had the longest race of all to run, and they had to do it on their own.

The educational systems of the UK and the USA
Administrative structure
There are slight variations in the educational system within the four countries of the UK, but generally they are similar. Much of the discussion of the UK educational system in this study relates specifically to England.

The compulsory educational system is more centralised in England than in the USA, although administration is done through local authorities (LA's). In England, much of the funding for education is paid for locally from council tax, although central government also contributes funds via these authorities. The USA's education system is more diverse, disparate and decentralised. Governmental authority for USA education lies more with each state than with Federal Government. The fifty states then delegate administrative responsibility to thousands of local school districts. The result is fifty systems of public, tax-supported lower and higher education in which policy is made by fifty sets of state officials, governors, legislatures, judges, state boards of education and their counterparts in thousands of local communities. The Federal Government provides significantly less funding to the education system than the UK government does.

Private education does exist in the UK but not at anywhere near the level of the USA. Widespread private institutions exist at every level in the USA, from nursery to higher education, whereas England has a significant number of private schools but far fewer private colleges and universities. In the USA, the overwhelming proportion of private sector schools are operated by religious denominations: Catholic, Lutheran, Episcopal, Seventh Day Adventist and Jewish being prominent among them. However, the most prestigious private schools are often non-sectarian.

School provision
Pre-school education has become increasingly widespread in both countries. In England, children start primary school at the age of 4 or 5. Most move into secondary school at the age of 11, but some will join a middle school before transferring to secondary school. Compulsory secondary education in the UK ends at the age of 16, but certain schools offer post 16 provision for two years in a sixth form. In the USA, formal schooling starts with elementary school at age 5. Children move into junior high and then high school until they reach 18.

Although both school systems are stratified, the UK's systems are more so, offering 'higher' and 'lower' curricula and awarding different kinds and levels of educational credentials (Allmendinger, 1989). Stratified systems differentiate among students at quite an early age and channel their access to educational opportunities further down the line. Secondary education credentials vary in the UK and include: GCSEs, GNVQs and A-levels, whereas in the USA there is only one qualification: the high school diploma. But the value of that diploma is often determined by the status of the school. School preparation for higher education takes place in all American high schools whereas in England, only some schools offer a sixth form.

By the time they reach secondary school, pupils in both the UK and the USA are generally tracked. Academic streaming generally begins at junior school (UK) and junior high (USA). In the UK, the streaming of pupils ultimately determines the tier students are put into for their GCSEs. All subjects have two streams except maths, which has three. The stream students are entered into for their GCSE determines the maximum grade they can achieve, so determining their future possibilities. Similarly, USA students planning to attend a four-year college are generally placed in an academic track where intense attention is paid to literature, foreign languages, higher mathematics, and sciences such as physics and chemistry. Pupils who do not do well in school are likely to be put into a middle track with a diluted academic curriculum. Upon graduation they may attend a community college or even a state college that does not have stringent entry requirements. Students may also be in a third track with a preponderance of vocationally oriented courses.

There is strong system-wide pressure for American students to obtain the high school diploma. The norms strongly promote college attendance in preference to post-secondary vocational courses, even though these are marketable in the labour force (Kerckhoff and Bell, 1998). USA students are faced with a choice of 'college or nothing', so many opt to pursue higher education.

Higher education

Access to university education in England is generally restricted to those who have gained certain academic credentials at secondary school, still generally A-levels. In the USA, however, any high school graduate is eligible to attend a community college at least. Undergraduate degrees in the UK normally run for three years and in the USA for four years.

In England, higher education (HE) is provided primarily by universities, although some colleges of further education provide higher education courses. Up until 1992 there were two main types of HE institutions: universities and polytechnics. In 1992 the polytechnics – and later many other colleges – were granted university status, although few of these new universities have the

same status as the traditional universities. Although there is a common perception that all universities in England are public institutions, this is not the
case. Many of the older Universities are in fact semi-private institutions, although all are highly dependent upon government funding. Students pay fees
towards their education and financial support is available for those who meet
the criteria. There are just over 100 HE institutions in the UK.

The USA has about 2,000 colleges and universities. Community colleges offer
two years of post-secondary education. Beyond this there are colleges and
universities that range from small four-year liberal arts institutions to huge
university systems. Institutions can be public or non-public. Community
colleges provide two years of academic coursework for students wanting to
transfer to a four-year liberal arts programme and generally require only
graduation from an accredited high school. Successful completion of a two-
year academic community college curriculum qualifies students for entry
into the upper division – the final two years – of a four-year college.

Structural characteristics of the educational systems

Kerckhoff *et al* (2001) revealed that a much larger proportion of English than
American students leave the educational system before the age of 18. Structural differences mean that fewer English than American students take a
post-secondary course, and English students take more vocational than
academic post-secondary courses. Far more students in the USA enter post-
secondary colleges and universities whereas more English students enter
vocational post-secondary schools (training centres and colleges of further
education) some of whom do progress into Higher Education. Although the
USA system includes vocational schools and community colleges, the
majority of students who take post-secondary courses go to four year colleges
because access to those colleges is much more open than is access to universities. Kerckhoff *et al* found that a much smaller proportion of English than
American students engaged in any kind of schooling between the ages of 23
and 28. However, in recent years, England has been encouraging young
people and adults to continue to study through national strategies such as the
government's Life Long Learning initiative.

Theoretical framework

Pierre Bourdieu's concept of cultural capital provides an overarching theoretical framework for my study as it offers an explanation for the reproduction
of educational inequality. It is a dominant theory, often used in an attempt to
construct explanations for differential educational achievement in a way that

combines a wide variety of influences. The term 'capital' has traditionally been used in connection with economics, but Bourdieu (1986) expands the notion beyond its economic conception to include social capital, a network of lasting social relations and sphere of contacts; symbolic capital, to include prestige, honour and the right to be listened to; and cultural capital, the collection of non-economic forces such as family background, social class, investments in and commitments to education and the different resources which influence academic success.

Cultural capital also refers to the role played by distinctive kinds of cultural tastes, knowledge, abilities, habits, attitudes and beliefs that are acquired primarily through socialisation in the process of class formations in contemporary societies. Bourdieu argued that cultural capital is of value in the academic market. The people endowed with much cultural capital tend to share similar accents, dispositions and learning, to have access to academic tools such as books and attend similar places of learning such as universities and libraries.

According to Bourdieu, education is mainly about social reproduction, serving the ideological purpose of enabling a dominant social class to reproduce its power, wealth and privilege legitimately. Hence whilst it may appear that everyone has an equal opportunity to succeed, this is not the case. The system is structured to favour one class over another. For Bourdieu, success is largely the preserve of pupils who are able to fit in with the dominant cultural values perpetuated through the school system. Bourdieu argues that a major role of schools is social elimination, that is, removing pupils from access to higher knowledge and social rewards. Elimination is achieved in two main ways. The first is through an examination system designed to progressively fail or exclude certain pupils, generally working-class pupils, whose cultural capital in examinations is seen to be less valid. Secondly, elimination is achieved through self-elimination, a practice prevalent amongst working-class children, who quickly come to understand that they don't speak the same language as the educational system, a system that offers them very little that is culturally useful. So they leave as soon as they can.

Bourdieu maintains that cultural capital is formed through nurture rather than nature. 'The initial accumulation of cultural capital, the precondition for the fast, easy accumulation of every kind of useful cultural capital, starts at the outset, without delay, without wasted time, only for the offspring of families endowed with strong cultural capital' (Bourdieu and Passeron, 1973).

According to Bourdieu, each economic class develops an associated 'class culture'. Ways of seeing the social world and ways of doing things within that world are developed out of the experiences of that class in the social world. He argues that children are not simply socialised into the values of society as a whole but also into the culture that corresponds to their class. These cultural experiences represents a form of cultural capital, that is, a set of values, beliefs, norms, attitudes, experiences that equip people for their life in society. Dominant cultural capital, held by those at the top of the economic strata, is more valuable than those held by less influential and powerful groups. Hence, for example, subtleties of language such as accent, grammar, spelling and style – all part of cultural capital – are a major factor in social mobility, affecting job opportunities and social status. The high value placed on the dominant cultural values that characterise the upper or ruling class is a reflection of their powerful position within society.

Through cultural reproduction, existing disadvantages and inequalities are passed down from one generation to the next, partly through the education system. Bourdieu and Passeron (1973) maintain that individuals do not enter the education market with equal amounts of capital or identical configurations; some already possess quantities of relevant capital bestowed upon them in the process of habitus formation during their upbringing. Their learned behaviour makes them better players than others in the field and their teachers recognise this.

Whilst the privileged children fit into the world of educational expectations with apparent ease, the unprivileged are found to be 'difficult' and to present 'challenges' – yet both behave as their upbringing dictates. Bourdieu regards this 'ease' or 'natural' ability as the product of great social labour, largely by the parents, to equip their children with the dispositions of manner and thought which ensure they are able to succeed within the educational system and can reproduce their parents' class position in the wider social system.

Are these successful boys really 'Black'?

The powerful influence of social capital invites the question: did these boys sell out their Blackness in order to be successful? Cultural ecological theories posit that Black students view education as a White person's activity and are therefore anti-education, so in order to succeed, Black students have to reject their Black identities and 'act White' (Fordham and Ogbu, 1986, 1998). Does this mean that the boys in this study had rejected their Black identities and thought and acted White?

The boys' desire to enhance their cultural knowledge

Many of the boys actively sought to strengthen their racial and cultural knowledge. Sometimes it was their parents who took the lead, actively seeking out information on their cultural heritage. These statements are typical: '*I have a good knowledge of Black people in history; my mum did a lot of research into this so I learnt a lot from her*' and '*mum and dad made us watch Roots and videos on people like Malcolm X*'. In other cases, the initiative sprang from the boys themselves. Some regularly surf the web for information of their culture, whilst others watched Black television programmes and videos and read books by Black authors.

The display of Black culture in their lifestyle

According to Ogbu (1992) Blacks in the USA have developed an oppositional cultural identity manifested in music (rap, hip-hop, jazz), through clothes (baggy, loose fitting) and even speech (Ebonics). As much of Black culture in the UK follows Black American culture, the same can be said of Black youth culture in the UK.

> An African poet once said 'I did not know I was Black until I came to America'. What that means to me is that being Black is partially socially constructed; it's a matter of how society reacts to you, not necessarily who you are. However, the way in which society reacts to you starts to form who you are, how you feel, how you react. I react by using slang and listen to certain types of music and I dance a certain way. I am from Detroit, so I kind of dress like I'm from the hood: baggy pants, gym shoes, etc. It is important because it is a means of distinguishing yourself, full stop. (Carver, Relay Boy, Harvard)

> If I was to change my skin colour to White and also change all my features which are associated with Black people, people could still tell that I was really Black from just the way I am: the way I speak, the way I dress, the way I dance, man, they would know, they would just know! They'd say there is something different about this guy, the food he eats, cos I'm into my patties and my hard dough bread. (Michael, Marathon Boy, Wolverhampton)

Some of the boys are so embroiled in Black culture that they feel that people could tell they were Black even if their skin colour and racial features changed to White. One said that it would be so obvious that he was really Black that people would describe him as '*a White chocolate*'.

Most were multicultural in their food preferences. They ate Chinese, Italian and the cultural dishes of the White indigenous population in which they lived, but Black traditional food remained central to their diets. The Muslim students would buy only from Halal shops. The Black Americans described their food as 'soul food': corn bread and ribs and, for the Haitian students, rice and chicken. The British students typically defined their cultural food as 'Black Man Food', the most popular dishes being: jerk chicken, ackee and salt fish, curry goat and rice and rice and peas.

> For my Sunday morning breakfast I'd have things like plantain, bammy and bacon and during the week I'd have things like stew peas and rice. (Jestin, Marathon Boy, Wolverhampton)

It was only in the area of food preferences that the UK students gravitated more towards their African or Caribbean cultural traditions than those in the USA. This might be because Black people have been settled in the USA for significantly longer so over time have become estranged from many of their traditional dishes.

Music plays a key part in people's identity and I found no difference in the music preferred. Both the British and American students liked R&B, rap and hip hop, and also gospel music. Many students confessed to being keen listeners to Black pirate radio stations. However, a few of the students also listen to classical music, jazz and soul music. The boys pointed out that it was not just their choice of music that distinguished them as Black but also, as one student put it, '*it's the way I listen to it as well i.e. with lots of bass*'.

Also significant were the students' clothes and their style of walk. Dressing, like music, is one activity that affirms colour in the Black community... just as speech is the measure of culture, so too is dress' (Edwards and Polite, 1992). Just over a quarter of the students referred to clothes as a means by which they expressed their cultural identity. But few claimed to have a culturally distinctive style of walk.

Edwards and Polite (1992) suggest that 'there is perhaps no surer indication of 'acting coloured' than 'speaking colour'; that is, speaking in the idioms, dialect, or slang associated with the Black class, the lower-class'. Several of the students could converse in a different dialect to their White majority peers – they tend to use slang and Black terms as well as a range of accents. As well as being able to 'speak colour' they could also speak the Queen's English. Edwards and Polite propose that to speak a language is to take on a world, and that to succeed in a White dominated culture, a Black person must take on the culture and language of that society and hence the 'Queen's' English.

> A lot of people wouldn't be able to tell that I am Black on the phone, especially if I put on my so called posh accent. (Bill, Marathon Boy, Oxford)

Many of the other students in this study could also code switch to an appropriate dialect depending on who they were conversing with. It is a skill they had mastered eloquently.

Many of the students said that their bedroom walls are covered with posters of Black people such as sports personalities and music stars like Missy Elliot. Some also collect cultural pictures, particularly African art. Their book collections typically feature cultural books and Black literature by or about Malcolm X, Martin Luther King and novels by Michael Dyson.

Relationships and associations

Most of the students expressed a preference for dating Black girls.

> When I was in middle school I was into White girls a lot, but as I got older, I got a sense of realness from a Black girl, 'this is my queen', and that's the way I look at it. With White girls, I just don't get that sense of devotion from them, it just seems that a Black girl is really there for you, they stick by you, you know; I just don't get that from a White girl. (Lester, Marathon Boy, Central Florida)

> For some reason, I cannot see myself with anybody except a Black woman. (Carver, Relay Boy, Harvard)

> I'm not racist you know but everyone has a preference and my preference is Black girls. (Brian, Marathon Boy, Central Florida)

The American students were more likely to date Black girls, perhaps because mixed racial relationships are more acceptable in the UK, where a trend towards this has emerged. But, there were also significant differences in their affiliations: far more the American students associated themselves with Black people and were politically active in the area of race.

> I was the head of my diversity group in high school, so went to the diversity meetings amongst the private school system on a regular basis. We did not have a Black association either in elementary or high school, but I was searching for something like this (the Black Men's Forum at Harvard). When I came for Pre frosh (an event for newcomers to Harvard) the Black Men's Forum had a real impact on me; there was a real sense of unity amongst the men. (Dillon, Sprinter Boy, Harvard)

> I was a prefect on the executive board of the student council and I challenged the school to deal with racial tensions; the Head has since made some positive changes. (Clive, Relay Boy, Harvard)

The American students displayed a strong sense of Black identity particularly at Harvard, where the Harvard Black Men's Forum founded by Black male students some years ago is still very strong today. Most of the Harvard students in this study are active members of the Forum. Like the students in Horvat and Lewis's study (2003), they wanted to be part of a Black community, a community they identified themselves with that strengthened their racial and cultural identity.

So was the question of whether these successful Black boys were really Black resolved? The answer is yes; the overwhelming majority of them were 'Black'; they were positive about their Blackness and they accepted and actively sought to know more about the positive and constructive aspects of their cultural heritage. In addition, most could be considered to be bi-cultural, embracing the positive aspects of the White dominated culture in which they lived in while embroiling themselves in a Black culture. According to Edwards and Polite (1992), embracing who they are provides an internal gyroscope that allows successful Blacks to function without getting emotionally or psychologically lost. These Black boys had not traded their Black identity for educational success. On the contrary, they sought to enhance it and doing so enabled them to operate from a position of racial strength.

PART TWO
OBSTACLES OVERCOME

2

The lens of social class

Social class is recognised as a significant structural impediment to academic achievement (Gunn *et al*, 1997). Since half the students in this study were from lower social class backgrounds it is a useful lens through which to view the social context in which Black boys are brought up and educated. Although some British researchers have claimed that social class has less effect on Black students than on White (Smith and Tomlinson, 1989; Department for Education and Skills, 2003), educational achievement is still strongly correlated with social class. This chapter seeks to establish whether any of the successful students in this study who were from lower social class backgrounds were exposed to the adverse characteristics associated with children brought up in underprivileged economic and social circumstances.

Carver

Carver, a USA Relay Boy from Harvard University, provides a useful case study. Many aspects of his social and economic experiences touch on key themes which emerged also from data collected from other students from underprivileged backgrounds. Carver gives a vivid description of the City of Detroit, the neighbourhood in which he spent his school years:

> I thought that the whole world looked like my neighbourhood until the day when I went over to one of my White friend's house. It was amazing, it was so clean, the grass was green, it was a big house. Then I started asking why it is that my neighbourhood looks the way it is. I saw the correlation between the quality of a neighbourhood and race. A lot of people will actually move away from Detroit because of the lack of entertainment and because there are no malls in Detroit, we have to go outside the city a lot, because the malls are all in the suburbs. It is kind of funny

though, because as soon as you leave Detroit you know that you are out of Detroit because, for one, things look nicer, and two, you start seeing White people. Also, as you drive your car in Detroit there are a lot of pot-holes, but as soon as you get outside Detroit the roads are smooth; that's how ridiculous it is!

Largely, my hood was dilapidated, it was sort of crime infested; violence was there and drugs was there. Detroit is one of the most segregated cities in the nation. I think the city is about 85 per cent Black and my high school is about 95 per cent Black, even though it was one of the best schools...

It was kind of a good neighbourhood until violence and drugs erupted. There were three major gangs in the hood; they were called 'Folks', 'Head Bangers' and 'The Blood'. I could remember hearing gunshots every night, but I wasn't afraid; it sort of seemed commonplace. Even though my grandmother and cousins lived a few blocks away from our home, my parents pretty much kept me confined to our block. I couldn't go too far down the street one way or too far down the other way. They kept a close eye on us; they made sure that we only associated with certain people in the hood.

I remember one time, our house got shot at. My parents used to rent out certain parts of our house as we have a two-family flat. They rented the house out to a single mother; she had a lot of kids. She had this boyfriend, who I think sold drugs and was indebted to the drug dealer; he would spend time at the house, and I guess the drug dealer thought it was his house so they drove by and shot it up. After that, my parents stopped renting the house and just allowed members of my family to stay.

I can remember times when the police would come on our block and do drug busts. The police would turn up in a van, one would come out, knock on a door, and then the rest of the police would come out of the back of the van. They would bring out people from their house and have them on their stomachs with their hands behind their back.

I still managed to stay out of that, and I never really had problems with any of the kids in the hood either. I was a friendly kid. They would come round to my house and play with my toys. Still, even today, I know that some of the kids are the ones who are in the gangs; but I saw goodness in them; I think there is intrinsic goodness in every single person. Eventually the gang thing sort of got out of control and a lot of people got killed. A lot of people ended up moving away, so the whole neighbourhood dynamics changed. My parents started being less involved in the community and I started spending less time with the kids in my neighbourhood...

Next to my house, I remember, the family moved out; it became abandoned and someone set it on fire. There are lots of houses like that in my area. The city [the State authorities] would often come in and just destroy the houses because the infrastructure had become so dilapidated that no one could live in it...

But now, I don't really like my little brother going outside, because he is a different kind of person than I am. I could handle myself in that sort of environment. People would look at me and not necessarily say 'there's a nerd, let's beat him up' or 'let's take advantage of him'. My brother isn't street smart; I can see him being picked on, and that's something that I don't want, so even when he does go outside, I keep a close eye on him...

The feeling in the hood was that in a lot of schools, their children were not supported; schooling was seen just as a babysitting place. I remember one time, the police brought this little kid out in handcuffs and threw him in the in the back of the police car.

At school we didn't have proper resources; I can recall being cold in class because we didn't have any heating. Some classes were held in the basement of the science centre museum, but the advantage was that when we got out of the basement we would have free access to the science centre museum. We did not have a gym because it was so small so we would have our gym [classes] in the hallway. For recess we would have to go outside and play in the parking lot, but it was good fun...

A lot of them [teachers] were good, some of them weren't. Some of them just couldn't control the class and some didn't have prepared lessons; some were just inadequate in my opinion. I remember this one class – the Spanish class in high school – the teacher could not control the class at all, so that whole year of Spanish was just a waste. But you've got to understand that teaching in a Detroit public school was hard, just because of the lack of educational resources, the pay, and the environment that they were in; they had to deal with all of this. I think the best teachers were the ones who acted like your mamma that wouldn't let you act up, that would encourage you and embrace you like your mamma; and like I said, a lot of teachers were Black females so we had a lot of those mothers.

It was good when we had a Black male teacher, a Black male teacher that was strong, a Black male teacher that was intelligent, because we didn't have many Black male role models in my neighbourhood or even in the school system. But some of the Black male teachers that we had weren't good, they weren't strong, they couldn't control the class. I remember this one bad teacher in middle school, he couldn't control the class, he'd loose papers, and he was timid.... in middle school, what is there to be timid about? But there was this other teacher we had in 10th grade, his name was Mr Taylor. He was strong, a young man, so someone we could relate to; he was funny, laid-back, and strong and very, very intelligent, so we enjoyed his class.

The physical landscape

The physical landscape of Carver's neighbourhood was characterised by dirt, dilapidated houses and pot-holed roads. Several other students described their neighbourhood as a 'ghetto neighbourhood'. They lived in *'very low-*

income government housing' in the USA and in *'large blocks of council flats'* in the UK. However, a few students such as Tawanda, a UK Marathon Boy from Wolverhampton University, said that his neighbourhood was *'typically a Black and ethnic minority area; it wasn't like rubbish though, but it could have been improved a lot'*. Tawanda's defence of his neighbourhood – that is was not 'like rubbish' – cropped up time and time again amongst the respondents. Although they recognised the deprivation of their neighbourhoods, they nonetheless felt a strong sense of affinity to them. Both Carver's and Tawanda's neighbourhoods were predominantly Black. Indeed, this was a key characteristic of the neighbourhoods of over three quarters of the students from lower-class backgrounds. In some cases, not only were their neighbourhoods one hundred per cent Black, but their surrounding areas were too.

The absence of shopping malls, as Carver noted, raised issues about economic regeneration, or rather the lack of it. Other students such as Delaney, a USA Marathon Boy from Harvard University, also drew attention to the lack of economic regeneration in his neighbourhood, characterised by *'a lapse of businesses, high levels of unemployment and a lot of young people roaming the streets'*.

The social landscape

Just over half the students from lower-class backgrounds were brought up in single family households. One student noted that his family was one of only two families in his immediate neighbourhood with both parents living together. With the exception of one of the UK student from a single family home, they all lived with their mothers.

Nearly half the students from lower-class backgrounds lived in neighbourhoods similar to Carver's, characterised by high crime levels, drugs and violence. Vincent described an incident in his neighbourhood, one which is renowned for rioting.

> Ely has a bit of a reputation; it is quite rough. They've had some riots there and one of them was very close to my school. The riot started quite small near our local chip shop and then the fighting just escalated. Basically just thousands and thousands of people were fighting in the streets, throwing petrol bombs etc. (Vincent, Relay Boy, Oxford)

As well as the riots, Vincent observed several adverse incidents in his neighbourhood including the stabbing of his friend's father and the involvement of people he knew in car thefts. Other students also talked about the activities of some of their peers in their neighbourhood. Jakim, for example, remembers:

> My friends became really bad; lots of them got locked up. It seems like everyone who went to Seven Sisters turned out bad; some got locked up for attempted murder, selling drugs etc. Their reputation was based on crime. In Haringey, you don't hear about people being smart, you hear about them being the strongest and the 'badest'. Smart people couldn't look down on my friends like Carlton, because he was bad. Carlton was 'cool'. To hang around Carlton you had to be cool. Carlton was king of the pack. It felt good to have Carlton as your friend. (Jakim, Marathon Boy, Wolverhampton)

Other students described their neighbourhood as being '*mashed down with lots of prostitutes*' and '*a danger zone*' with '*lots of crime, shooting, fighting*' which required them having to '*develop certain skills in order to survive*'. However, like Carver, despite the negative features of their environment, they still felt '*safe*' and undisturbed by the incidents in their neighbourhood.

> It has a reputation for being a rough area, yes it has its little scuffles and that, but I don't think it's a rough area. I think people regard it as a rough area because it has a high proportion of ethnic minorities there. (Julieus, Marathon Boy, Wolverhampton)

A quarter of the students recalled fond memories of their neighbourhood: '*It was a poor area but it was a happy area*', '*there was a strong community*' and '*everyone knew each other, we all grew up together, and there was a good social network*'. Trevor, who grew up in a poverty stricken neighbourhood, said:

> The neighbourhood I lived in was very friendly; it's very much like those neighbourhoods you see on TV all the time with old ladies who gave you treats, kids playing out on the streets and all that kind of stuff. It was a tightly knit neighbourhood. (Trevor, Marathon Boy, Central Florida)

Carver identified the strong divide between the 'rich and poor' in Detroit, and Bill experienced a similar racial and class divide:

> Croydon is a massive borough, i.e. the biggest borough in London. You have the Surrey bit which is more middle-class, and the London bit, which is more like working-class with a very high percentage of Blacks. If you (a Black person) walked down the street, in the London bit, you feel like you are a majority. (Bill, Marathon Boy, Oxford)

With the exception of Brian, a USA Marathon Boy from Central Florida University who lived in a rural neighbourhood where most people worked in farming related areas, all the students from lower-class backgrounds lived in inner city urban areas. However, even in the rural area where there was little crime, Brian said '*it wasn't the kind of place where you would want to raise your kids; it wasn't well developed; it was a poor neighbourhood*'.

The social environment children are brought up in is often considered to be a key influence on their behaviour. We see in Carver's case that he was surrounded by crime: he witnessed drug raids, escaped the potentially fatal consequences of a drive-by shoot-out and was surrounded by friends who were involved in gangs. However, most of these students, like Carver, managed to avoid being adversely influenced by their social environment. But not all. A few admitted that they were not entirely innocent bystanders at incidents in their neighbourhoods. One confessed that he and his friends 'used to cause a bit of trouble there'. Others owned up to being 'influenced by the negative people around', and to being 'naughty in those days'. Lester recalls just how difficult being surrounded by such negative influences was for them.

> Just living were I lived, it was in your face every day; like just going down the street, you see people on the corner selling drugs, you see all the prostitutes, the crack heads. It's up to you to distinguish yourself from all of that. (Lester, Marathon Boy, Central Florida)

Not only were some of the students involved in criminal activities, but Trevor, told me that his mother was directly involved.

> My mum lived a bad life, a life of crime. She's been back and forth to prison over the years. I lived with my grandma; my dad stayed at a distance.

How these students overcame the adverse effects of their social landscape is discussed in Part Three of this book.

The educational standards in the neighbourhood

Areas which are characterised by structural inequalities, poor housing and high crime rates are often correlated with poor standards of education. Only one English and three American students described their schools as being 'average', 'good' or 'very good'. Carver's recollection of his school's standards appeared similar to many other students'. Most of the students from lower-class backgrounds described the standards and attainment level of the schools in their neighbourhood as 'poor'. Dumali, a Sprinter Boy who attended Harvard University, reported that there was a general consensus in his urban inner city neighbourhood that 'if the school is not in the suburbs then the standard needs to be brought up'. A number of these schools were described as 'run down', with 'poor facilities' and a 'shortage of resources', where 'kids were left to mess around'. Other students were more disparaging, describing their school, as 'rubbish', 'like a youth club'. More of the English students expressed such negative recollections of their schools. Vincent, for example, a Relay Boy who went to Oxford recalls:

The results of my school weren't good, to be honest. There were about 140 of us in year eleven and only 40 sat their GCSEs and only 20 of us got them. Our position in the league tables was pretty lame. There were about 30 schools in Cardiff and we were about 24th. No one took their GCSEs really seriously because no one told us how important they were. In fact all we heard was parents say that GCSEs are rubbish, they are not worth anything.

Vincent's mother, like many parents from lower-class backgrounds, felt they had little choice about sending their children to school in their immediate neighbourhood. Only one student wanted to stay in his neighbourhood, even though he knew standards were poor, because he wanted to stay local.

Albert was first schooled in the ghetto where he lived and then later in a middle-class neighbourhood when his parents moved to the suburbs after obtaining better jobs. Albert noticed the stark difference in the standards of the schools in the ghetto and those in the suburbs.

The teachers didn't put too much of an effort into their work. I guess it's because their income was low because they worked in a poor school. They didn't do much with the students; they really didn't care about certain things. But when I changed school, it was different. It was a nearly all White school and they had money so they made the teachers work for their money; it was a high performing school. (Albert, Sprinter Boy, Central Florida)

Not all the schools in the poor neighbourhoods were below standard however – a few neighbourhoods had both low and high performing schools with wide catchment areas. Bill, a Marathon Boy who attended Oxford University said:

In Croydon, you have some of the worst comprehensive schools. Two of the schools were failing schools. The school that my sister went to was poor. Almost two thirds of them had free school meals. It was under subscribed and had mainly ethnic minority children. Yet just across the road from that was one of the best independent schools in the country who featured in the top 100 schools. So if you could get your kid into a good school in that borough, they could do well. My brother went to a school that wasn't a good school, and it had a lot of children in there that just couldn't get into other schools. Many of my brother's friends who were Black got suspended, mostly for simple things like their haircuts.

Bill and a few other boys from single family households faced challenges at school because they were poor. He recalls:

Schools held the view that children with single parents had free school meals, and when they played rugby their mothers didn't come along, and that kind of thing. I had free school meals, but sometimes I would go without school meals because I was embarrassed about having to present my tokens to the dinner ladies in front of my friends. It was embarrassing enough to be in a queue where everyone was paying with money and you take out your token to pay for your meal, but it was even worse if you had to put things back because your token wasn't enough to pay for them. It got to a point where I didn't claim my token, I either made my own packed lunch at home or I starved. I didn't tell my mum that though. It was hard for my mum to come to Parents Evenings or to watch me play rugby, not only because of her physical health but also because she couldn't drive. I would feel embarrassed about getting freebies for trips. The school probably knew we were poor because I never went on any school trips or anything like that. On one occasion my teacher was prepared to waive the £100 fee for me to go on a trip abroad but I felt so embarrassed so I got my mum to ring and say I was too ill to come. (Bill, Marathon Boy, Oxford)

Michael, a Marathon Boy who went to Wolverhampton University said:

All my friends had designer clothes and the latest trainers and this and that, but we couldn't afford them. It was just my mum, I didn't have a father. Some kids had £5 pocket money; I had nothing. I didn't understand it then, but now I do; she had it hard.

Bill drew attention to the adverse impact of poor neighbourhoods on the career aspirations of students:

No one on my street was a doctor or a lawyer. The only professionals we knew of were teachers at school – and you would never want to be a teacher – or our doctor who we saw occasionally. There were no role models in our neighbourhood neither did we ever have any interaction with professionals, unlike those who came from middle-class backgrounds; that's why their expectations are higher.

Concluding remarks

One should not overlook the wider structural issues associated with educational attainment. The insight students offered into the environments in which they lived their daily lives sheds some light on the complex social problems confronting them and the potentially adverse impact on them and their education. Most of them lived in poverty stricken communities where educational standards were low, resources were scarce and where they were surrounded by environmental, moral and social degradation.

The poor education of many parents and the socially and economically deprived conditions experienced by many students constantly in their neighbourhoods and at school invites the question: How did these students respond to their circumstances in ways that allowed them to achieve academic success? The answer to this and other questions raised in Part Two of the book are discussed in Part Three.

3

The parents' involvement

Black parents are often pathologised for the educational underachievement of their sons. Whether this is justifiable is another matter (see Chapter 6), but it is a common perception among teachers. They regard Black parents as being indifferent to their sons' education, an assumption based largely on their 'invisibility' in school. And they see the absence of Black fathers in the home as a factor in Black boys' underachievement. This chapter engages with the discourse on parental involvement in a bid to determine whether the parents of students in this study exhibited the characteristics associated with parents who are pathologised for the underachievement of their children.

Inadequate Involvement
Just less than a quarter of the respondents said that they did not get any direct educational support in the home from their parents.

> I didn't get a lot of help at home. I went to nursery from [aged] one. They were working parents. I would come home at 4pm and there was no one home until 6.30. Every day my mum would ring home to make sure that I was home and had locked the door. She'd instruct me to go upstairs and to make some tea and toast. By the time she got in, I would have had my bath and was ready for bed. (David, Marathon Boy, Oxford)

> My mum just talked to me about the importance of education, but she wasn't in a position to help me because she didn't have an education. They didn't buy any books or anything like that to help me. (Brian, Marathon Boy, Central Florida)

All these parents except two had had poor education.

There is a notable difference between the support parents give their sons during elementary school and subsequent years, when their involvement declined markedly or even stopped altogether. This pattern is evident in the experiences of over half the boys whose parents had initially been involved in their education and is especially true amongst those from the USA, single mothers, parents whose own education had been poor, and those from poor socio-economic backgounds. The decline in parental support is often explained as being constrained by time:

> Mum became less active when my dad left and she became the bread winner. (Clive, Relay Boy, Harvard)

> I got help in elementary school but not after that because mum was working two jobs ... not a chance of getting help with school work. (Rob, Marathon Boy, Central Florida)

The support of some of the less privileged declined steadily because their own knowledge base was inadequate. In secondary school, children venture into new subject areas, of which many parents have little if any knowledge.

> My parents didn't really help me as much after 7th grade, because it got too hard for them, so I did it on my own. (Semore, Relay Boy, Harvard)

A correlation was also found between parental involvement and parents' level of confidence in their son's ability to do well:

> By the time I got to high school I knew pretty much what I was doing, but at elementary school she was there with me when she got off work she would help with my homework and do all that for me. (Bobzy, Relay Boy, Central Florida)

Parent's evenings

Attendance at Parents Evening or Parent Teacher Association meetings is another major aspect of parental involvement which is exalted by teachers (Crozier, 2000). A quarter of the parents in this study did not attend. The reasons given by their sons for this were clear:

> My parents didn't go to PTA meetings because they did not believe in it. They felt that they could adequately affect my education by checking on me rather than going to PTA meeting. (Dumali, Sprinter Boy, Harvard)

Others chose not to attend because they found these meetings unproductive. This mismatch between parents' and teachers' expectations of these meetings is as marked – as it was in Vincent's (1996) and Blair and Bourne's (2002) studies.

> My parents never went to parents evenings. My father came to one parents' evening in year seven. They believed they were a waste of time because they only got five minutes with a teacher. They said if there was a problem they would see my teacher, and they did. (Henroy, Sprinter Boy, Oxford)

Parents who did attend these events sometimes found the experience negative.

> Mum likes the good teachers, she can tell who the good teachers are, cause they are the ones who sit down with her at parents' evening for 45 minutes talking about me. Some teachers didn't expect me to do well, they would spend 5, 10 minutes with my mum at parents' evening. Its like my English teacher, she didn't like me at all. We could see she just wasn't interested; we just wanted to go home. (Michael, Marathon Boy, Wolverhampton)

Michael is aware that the teachers who had a positive attitude towards him were the ones who were positive towards his mother.

There is much synergy between the findings of this study and Blair and Bourne's study (1998). They too found that some Black parents find Parents Evenings unproductive. Parents in their study complained that teachers only seem to want to focus on their son's behaviour, rather than giving rounded feedback. They were critical of the general blanket progress report teachers give, telling them, '*your son is doing fine*', when this is not reflected in the marks. Parents reported being '*fobbed off*' when they do visit the school and being treated with disrespect when they want to take up some issues. They complained about being '*talked down to*' by teachers and generally treated as second-class citizens because of their colour and class.

Absent fathers

Although highly contested by researchers such as Francis and Skelton (2005), researchers such as Bleach (2000) point to the lack of positive male role models in the lives of boys, due in part to the break-up of families and the absence of fathers as a reason for the underachievement of boys. The parents of nearly one-fifth of the students in this study divorced while they were at school. One such student was David.

David – a vignette

> I was 15 when my dad left; mum was devastated, so I had to be strong. She had been with my dad for 20 odd years; they did everything together. When they started off they had very little ... but they worked hard, so by the time he left, we had two shops and a decent house. We were the perfect family; we had our own business, our own house, a flash car and we went on holiday three times a year. Then to come

home one evening and be told that my dad is leaving without any explanation, and then not to hear from him again for four years ... that was a lot to take in...

The whole experience spurred me on to prove to people that we could make it. We attended church and all of a sudden it was no longer two of my parents attending it, was only one. I knew people were talking and whispering about us, so I didn't want anyone to turn to my mum and say that I have gone off the rails since my dad left.

My books and my education was a way of getting away from all that. I would go into my room and all my books were there; everything I needed to improve myself was in that room. If I wasn't in there I was at the library. It made me more of a man, because it fell on me to provide support to my mum. The relationship between me and my mum now is very much a brother and sister relationship. She relies on me to decide what to do next, where to go on holiday, to say 'this guy is nice you know, give him a chance' (David, Marathon Boy, Oxford)

David is one of the students who was a rebel before turning himself around shortly before his father left. David not only lost his male role model in the home after his father left, but his standard of living dropped drastically. And all this happened at a critical time in his schooling, just before his final GCSE year. Yet this devastating change in his life accelerated his maturity. He strove to support his mother both financially and morally, and the responsibility he assumed spurred him on to focus on his education as a means of escaping from the pain of loss and upheaval.

Other students shared their experiences of the break-up of their families, typically describing it as '*devastating*'. But none of them reacted as David did. They became disengaged from school and their morale and their attitude towards schoolwork plummeted still further when for example their mother found a new partner or had a baby with another man. One student said that it wasn't until '*things came to a head*' with his common-law stepfather, that his mother finally sat him down and had a '*heart to heart*' talk before things began to improve at home. The resentment the boys felt was not just towards their mothers' new partners but often also towards the fathers who had left them.

Other students became estranged from their fathers, albeit to a lesser extent, for an entirely different reason: the fathers' over-employment.

During my childhood, my dad used to work crazy hours, including Christmas Day. We used to have to get up like 4am in the morning to open up presents before he went to work. (Semore, Relay Boy, Harvard)

> When I was young, I often didn't see him; he used to work some mad shifts, so we were never close. It wasn't until I started to go to senior school that we started to have some form of a relationship; now it's strong but it took a long time to get that close. He has always been proud of me and everything, but we never really spoke. It was me and mum. (Fabian, Relay Boy, Wolverhampton)

> I knew that my dad was working so he could pay for all the stuff that we were enjoying. (Wilton, Sprinter Boy, Harvard)

Such long working hours and time away from home affected the relationship of certain fathers with their sons. It also helps to explain why some of the fathers were not directly involved in their sons' education.

Concluding remarks

This study reveals that many of the factors associated with the parents of Black boys who underachieve are also evident amongst some of the parents of these successful students. A significant number of them had no father figure in the home for all or part of their school years, whether because of family break-up or, less often, because the fathers were at work for long hours every week. Some parents did not attend Parents Evenings or Parent Teacher Association events, and many provided little, if any, educational support to their sons. Those who did give some support gave progressively less as the boys advanced through school.

All this is contrary to the discourse on parental involvement in children's education. This claims that parental involvement entails help with school work and regular attendance at schools, particularly at Parents Evenings. The parents who do not comply are pathologised as being disengaged from their children. The concept of parental involvement is certainly not unproblematic. Tomlinson's studies (1991 and 1992) support the findings from this study about the constraints of Black parents' involvement in the education of their children. Whilst some had little choice about attending Parents Evenings, others made an informed decision not to attend because they found them unproductive.

When examining the relationship between teachers and Black parents through the lens of social class, it becomes evident that social class relations impact upon parent school relations. Parents from lower classes were noticeably more distant from and marginalised by the school than the middle-class parents, who had greater confidence about interacting with the school. Interestingly, Connell *et al* (1982) postulate that any parent/school relationship is a contest for domination of one by the other, and Giddens (1991) argues that events such as Parents Evenings serve as a mechanism for allowing teachers to display their expertise in a controlled manner. Whilst the contest between the middle-class parents and the teachers is fairly equally balanced, the contest between the working-class parents and the teachers is not. Being aware of this imbalance, working class parents tend to opt out of the contest. Yet although some of the Sprinter boys' parents who did not attend Parents Evenings did engage with the school at other times, it was they, not the school, who decided when to engage with the school.

The constraints on their time that many parents face today is a recurring theme of this study. The traditional model of parental involvement is of the middle-class housewife and mother who has unlimited time to support her elementary age child's homework activity. But this is a wholly inappropriate picture of many Black parents, particularly single parents and many parents who work full time who have little time to provide the kind of support teachers expect. Furthermore one cannot ignore the fact that a high proportion of Black families are single parent households, headed mostly by working mothers. This pattern applied to many students in this study. Single parents face pressure to do everything that is expected of a 'good' parent – single-handed. This seems to be exemplified in the USA where many parents have to hold down more than one job in order to make ends meet.

The general decline in parental involvement once their sons reached secondary/high school revealed in this study points to a probable correlation with the downward trend of underachievement at secondary school. There are, however, valid reasons for this decline. For example, the educational backgrounds of parents determined their knowledge and confidence to support their sons as they moved up the school.

The type of parental involvement in the education of their sons so often required by teachers demand time, resources and knowledge of the subject being taught. Given that most of the parents of the students in this study did not possess these assets, the traditional model of parental involvement is inapplicable. If the traditional notion of a good parent is applied to the parents considered in this study, then most would not be considered to be 'good' parents in the educational context. However, the fact that these students have been successful in their educational pursuits compels the examination of other interweaving aspects of their parenting. A more comprehensive picture is needed. For example, did these parents engage in practices which compensated for their perceived 'disengagement' from the education of their sons? This and related questions are addressed in Chapter 6

4

Racism and Racial Identity

Racism in school has long been deemed to contribute to the under-achievement of Black pupils. One theory is that it is due to the personal racism of White pupils, and of teachers who hold stereotypical views about them, treat them differently and have low expectations of them, that Black pupils do poorly (Sewell, 1997; Blair *et al*, 1998; Judd, 1999; Ofsted, 1999; DES, 2003).

A second theory attributes the cause of academic failure to institutional racism: where rules, formal procedures, regulations and informal practices have the effect of discriminating against members of an ethnic group (CRE, 1985; Macpherson, 1989). In the context of schools, institutional racism is usually manifested through their failure to tackle racism (Hopkins, 1997; Hamilton *et al*, 1999; O'Leary and Betts, 1999; Majors, 2001).

Closely related to these theories about racism are racial identity quandary theories. They too seek to explain Black boys' underachievement, but focus on the boys themselves and how they self-manage the effects of being a minority in a White dominated society. They argue that the pupils have developed low self esteem (Osborne, 1997) in response, and experience tensions between maintaining their Black identity and 'acting White' (Fordham and Ogbu, 1986) as well as tensions between their endeavours to perform academically whilst meeting the demands of their peers (Majors and Billson, 1992).

This chapter examines whether the students in this study encountered racism or experienced quandaries over racial identity. Or were they exempt from these factors which are purported to undermine the academic achievement of Black boys?

Racism
Pupil racism

Most students in this study were frequently on the receiving end of racism from other pupils. Tony's experiences were typical:

> I was bullied at school because I was Black, because I was tall, because I was good at sport ... and I wasn't going to be quiet and shy away. My House Master didn't know what was going on so I got into lots of trouble; my mum had to come and save me. On one occasion, a boy at my school chased me around a table with a knife because he didn't like me; he got expelled. On another occasion, a group of older boys verbally abused me. Sometimes when I played rugby with other schools I was racially abused. Even just walking down the streets in Lancaster, I got racially abused. Once someone pulled up in a car, rolled down his window and just hurled racial abuse at me. (Tony, Sprinter Boy, Oxford)

However, Tony's perception of being targeted because of his sporting ability is not a common perception amongst the students in this study; on the contrary, most felt that being good at sport prevented them from being bullied. In standing up to the bullies, Tony found himself in trouble with the school authorities, who were insensitive to the racial context of his reactive behaviour so failed to address the underlying issue. Only intervention by his parents enabled Tony to survive at that school.

Students involved in this study were commonly called abusive names like *'nigger' 'blackie'*, *'you Black bastard'* and even *'paki'* and were subjected to racist jokes. Numerous studies have identified name calling as the commonest manifestation of racism in schools (Troyna and Hatcher, 1992; Gaine, 1995; De Lima, 2001; Sibbitt, 1997). In addition, students appeared to be vulnerable when the subject of race came up in class, eliciting behaviour such as *'kids drawing pictures of a gollywog'*. These students put up with a great deal, but found certain things intolerable. Sam, for example, said:

> I could accept when people called me nigger and that, but when they started to refer to my colour as being dirty, that really got to me. (Sam, Marathon Boy, Wolverhampton)

Most of the boys felt *'offended'* by any form of racial remarks; they *'hated being disrespected'*. Although a few regarded racist remarks as *'only silly comments'* and chose to ignore them, most did not take kindly to any form of racist abuse. One student who had long ignored it, finally threatened his abusers, because he felt that *'if I didn't, I would be disrespecting myself too'*. Others felt the need to *'sort things out there and then'*. One boy told me that *'racism made me feel angry; it was grounds for a fight.'* Others responded by doing things like '*sticking a pencil in his arm*'. But when students retaliated, as Tony did, they found themselves on the wrong side of the school authorities and ended up with detention or even suspension.

The racism took the form of not only verbal abuse but also more subtle stereotyping. Some of the boys felt that their White friends had '*low expectations*' of them and were at first '*surprised that I got good grades*'. Hugh sums up some of the covert racial undertones that laced his day to day interactions with some of his schoolmates:

> There were a lot of kids who didn't like me because I am Black, but I couldn't say that, because they wouldn't say it. You know that they know that you know that they don't like you because of your colour but nothing would be done about it because they were too smart to say so. (Hugh, Sprinter Boy, Oxford)

The DfES (0416/2004) report acknowledges that the academic progress of pupils who are on the receiving end of racist name-calling and racist bullying can be severely damaged. The report highlights the fact that pupils rarely reported racist incidences and suggest that this is connected to the perception amongst pupils and parents that staff would be unable or unwilling to take appropriate action. But as can be seen from Hugh's experience, racism can also manifest in subtle ways which cannot always be classified as an incident.

Parents' racism

A few of the students also encountered racism from the parents of other pupils.

> I wasn't treated differently by the teachers, but I got it from the children and even the parents. One parent even swore at me. I didn't get upset though when they called me a Black bastard, I just dealt with it in my own way. (Tawanda, Marathon Boy, Wolverhampton)

> As [we] got older there was a division in our friendship; I guess, the prejudices of his parents had finally taken place within him. When you're younger, things like skin colour doesn't matter; what may matter is whether or not you stink. (Carver, Relay Boy, Harvard)

> With the parents I had to prove myself. My friends would ask their parents if it was okay to invite me to the house. My friends accepted me but their parents were another story. But once they realised I wasn't going to deal drugs or shoot-up the school, then I was okay. (Clive, Relay Boy, Harvard)

But Tawanda's experience of direct racial abuse from parents was rare. Generally the parents display subtle racist attitudes and stereotyping although one student heard his parents being called '*monkey*' by other parents. The cases cited concerned White parents from lower-class backgrounds.

Teacher racism

Nearly half the students said they had to face racism from their teachers at some point during their schooling. One remembers being called a '*monkey*' by his teacher, and another reported that his teacher openly confessed in front of the class that she didn't like him because of his colour. Overt verbal racism from teachers was, however, very rare. Racism was usually manifested in more covert ways such as the low expectations of Black boys.

> The teachers I found frustrating were the ones who expected less of you. I found that being the only Black person in all of my classes hard; some teachers reacted negatively towards me. (Hugh, Sprinter Boy, Oxford)

Other students confirmed that teachers' expectations were low: '*some teachers were surprised when you did well, they did not expect Black children to be bright; they found it shocking*' and '*my teachers were certainly shocked that they had two Black children in their school that were cleverer than most of the other children*'. These expectations were linked with racist teachers' stereotypical views.

> I never knew that I was smart until I left the private (predominately White) school. At that school, the only expectation they had of me was for me to become an athlete, whereas at the public (predominantly Black) school, my teachers would encourage me and congratulate me for my academic achievements. The attention that I got from being intelligent was positive; I even got accolades from the Principle. (Carver, Relay Boy, Harvard)

The boys also observed that teachers were '*more likely to point a finger at the Black children first*', and were '*quicker to discipline the Black children than the White children*'.

> Teachers at school saw us (the Black boys) as dumb time wasters. Sometimes they actually told lies about me; they blamed me for things I did not do. Once I got blamed for stealing a walkman; it had nothing to do with me, in fact I wasn't even around school during the time of the incident. They had simply stereotyped me and made me out to be bad when I wasn't. Yeah, I may have gone to a grammar school, but it's not the type of school you go to that's important. I know of kids who didn't go to good schools yet they did well at school. My school had a high educational standard, but I didn't do well in that school because of racism. (Sean, Relay Boy, Wolverhampton)

Sean underachieved at school, not only by grammar school standards but also by national standards set by the UK Government. Sean perceived there to be a direct link between racism in school and his underachievement. It wasn't until he left school and enrolled at college where the environment was more conducive to his learning that he obtained the credentials to move up the educational ladder.

Another common form of racism which emerged from this research was the differential treatment the boys received from teachers. They observed that *'some teachers don't pay much attention to Black boys'*, that they *'favoured Whites over Blacks ... and it was obvious'*. Another American student, like Carver, said he was glad when he moved from a predominantly White school to a predominately Black one because he got more attention there. There are other examples of differential treatment such as being *'talked down to at times'*, being *'overlooked for playing certain roles in school plays'* and over-looked for receiving awards which they believed they deserved.

Over 20 per cent of the students articulated examples of institutional racism.

> In my 8th grade, a guy called me a monkey, so I kinda hit him in the face. He didn't get into trouble for that but I got into big trouble from the teachers; I got a day in-school suspension for it. (Semore, Relay Boy, Harvard)

> At primary school I used to be racially bullied, but the dinner ladies ignored it and my teachers dismissed it. (Synesius, Sprinter Boy, Oxford)

The students regarded such experiences in their school lives as critical. They left them feeling alienated in school. Some parents gave their sons moral support at a distance and others dealt directly with the issue. One boy remembers his mother going to his school on several occasions to meet with the head-teacher, but this had made him feel even more alienated and defenceless, because *'little was done about it'* and eventually his mother *'gave up'* trying. Some parents resorted to instructing their sons to *'stand up'* to the racist children rather than challenging or coercing the school to deal with institutional racism. Retaliation often put the boys on the wrong side of the school authorities; for many, it became a vicious circle.

Institutional racism

The under-representation of Black teachers in schools has been held up as a by-product of institutional racism. Although the staffing composition of the boys' schools is unknown, most had few if any Black teachers, particularly in the UK. So it is reasonable to surmise that most, if not all of the students attended schools where Black teachers, and specifically Black male teachers were under-represented. There were significantly more Black teachers and Black headteachers and administrators in the USA, because it has a far larger

Black population than the UK and, moreover, encourages affirmative action, and so gives preferential treatment to certain groups of people that are under-represented in the teaching profession.

Institutional racism is subtly manifested in teachers' lack of understanding of the cultures of Black children. That they were ill-equipped to teach Black children is picked up by some of the students:

> In my school I was the only Black person. There were some teachers who didn't know how to relate to you. Whenever race issues came up they felt uncomfortable. I always felt in the middle of it all, so I tended to withdraw from the discussion. (Sam, Marathon Boy, Wolverhampton)

> How clueless some of these White teachers can be. (Neil, Sprinter Boy, Harvard)

Students expressed their disappointment that their culture was not reflected in the curriculum.

> I've gone through the education system though to Oxford but I never studied Black history, I never studied a Black author, I've never studied any Black philosophers, I never did any form of Black music; they don't value you. Maybe if Black boys had the opportunity to study these things they would be more interested in education, it would engage them. (Bill, Marathon Boy, Oxford)

> I read some Black literature on my own and whilst I was reading it I felt that this could really be incorporated into the curriculum. (Delaney, Marathon Boy, Harvard)

> I chose to do African American studies at university because I wasn't taught it at school and I love our culture and everything about it: the music, the art, the poetry, the literature. (Trevor, Marathon Boy, Central Florida)

The few who had been taught culturally related lessons in school tended to be critical about their quality and content. The lessons tended to focus on slavery. The time devoted to such subjects was also criticised, as Erick relates:

> It would have been nice to have studied other things apart from slavery, subjects that were a bit more positive. I know Black soldiers contributed to the Second World War and that there's lots of figures in British history, where Black people have done positive things, like composing music. It would have been nice to hear about them and what they have done rather than the slave trade and how terrible it was. It's about getting a balance. We need an acknowledgement of Black people's contribution to this country. (Erick, Marathon Boy, Oxford)

Institutional racism was cited equally by students on both sides of the Atlantic, but except for one student, all were from Harvard and Oxford and had attended predominantly White schools.

Quandaries about racial identity

Children, particularly during adolescence, seek to establish their identity. Many Black children living in White dominated societies struggle with a particular aspect – their racial identity. About a third of the students in the study talked about the multifaceted struggles they faced in coming to terms with their own racial identity, maintaining or rejecting that identity, and struggling to 'fit' into the dominant society.

Henroy: a vignette

Henroy lived in a little village just outside Bristol and his was the only Black family in the village.

> At secondary school, for the first two years, people use to pass me and say 'hey man' or 'get off me man' and I'd think 'What?'; I hated it. It's as if there are Black people from Black land where they do Black things, like there's something unique about being Black that makes you do 'Black things'. I like being almost fully naturalised, but I am an English person in England, and I do what the English people do. When I am in Ghana I do what the Ghanaians do.

> ... It's partly the way I was brought up. My mother was keen that I was not stereotyped. She use to say things like 'it might not be fair, but people will think you are X, Y or Z when you might not be', and 'Black people stereotype themselves, but it's not worth living up to what the media portrays you as; so nothing in your hair, nothing patterned'. I have become some sort of a transplantation of a Black person in a White country, so I'm Black but English in every thing I do.

> ... There are so many things which I do which are not English by virtue of the fact that I was brought up in a Ghanaian family. My diet is not English at all, rice and stews, but at the same time, I am the product of being brought up with White children both in primary and secondary schools. I like to think that I am a product of how I have been brought up rather than a product of a culture that has been enforced on me because of the colour of my skin. I speak the way people spoke around me. I'm not ashamed to be English and I'm definitely not ashamed to be Ghanaian. One of the things I regret is not being able to speak my father's language. I'm conscious that even though I was born here I am an immigrant in this country because I stick out. I don't feel that I have a home in as much as I am an immigrant over here, and yet when I go to Ghana, people know I am English by the way I talk, walk etc. I don't feel I have a real home; I don't feel I come from anywhere. In Ghana, it's obvious that I'm not Ghanaian and in Britain, it's obvious that I'm not English, but I want to be both.

This vignette highlights some of the tensions Black boys feel about their racial identity. To foster his success, Henroy's mother steered him away from aspects of his Black identity that she feared would work against him. However,

Henroy still felt he needed to belong to both cultures, even though he felt rejected by both England and Ghana. Tensions of this kind were far more noticeable amongst the British students. Jestin, a Marathon Boy from Wolverhampton University, regarded himself as Black British until his adolescence, when he consciously chose to describe himself as African Caribbean, despite being born in England. As he put it: '*I don't see myself as British. I don't feel accepted here, unlike when I go to Jamaica on holiday; it feels like home. So I don't refer to myself as Black British anymore*'. This lack of sense of belonging in the UK was shared by many of the boys.

Even Sam, who is mixed race, eventually came to feel the same way as the students whose parents were both Black.

> I don't feel that I'm British even though I was born and brought up here. I don't feel any sense of patriotism towards Britain. That's just how I feel and I don't think that's personal to me. In Bangor, everyone considered me to be Black even when I tell them I have a White parent, they still consider me to be Black. (Sam, Marathon Boy, Wolverhampton)

Tensions over racial identity were apparent in other ways. Tony, for example, reflects on the process he went through before coming to terms with his racial identity:

> My whole identity about being Black has evolved over the years. When I was young, I was the only Black person around. I don't think I realised how much at the time, but it was quite awkward being Black. I used to think, how come I am Black and my parents are Black but everybody else is White, what's going on? But I remember at boarding school someone asking me if I wished I was White, but I answered 'no' because I didn't. The fact that I am Black is such a small part of me but at the same time it's a big part. When people see me they just see me as Black. But that tells you very little about me because I'm from Lancashire, and I went to boarding school, my parents are middle-class, I'm grammar school educated and I'm at Oxford. The fact that I am Black is important to me because it's who I am, but it's not the first thing about my identity which I consider to be important. I'm at a comfortable place of being Black. I associate with more Black people now than when I was younger, which is understandable because there weren't any other Black people around where I was brought up.(Tony, Sprinter Boy, Oxford)

The challenges the boys faced while coming to terms with their racial identity at times affected their behaviour. Whilst some students did not articulate the connection between these challenges and their behaviour, others, such as Alfred, did.

> Elementary to high school was fine but in my adolescent years I went off track. That was more to do with coming to terms with my cultural identity, being African and

being African American, and being American. I had a hard time trying to culturally identify myself and come to terms with who I was, which was important to me. It came into conflict with my education, whether studying was important or hanging out with my friends was more important, being a serious academic or not. Those types of decisions needed to be made, so it was a confusing time for me. Generally I started to perform badly on tasks, not studying what I should be studying, misbehaving, going out more, talking on the phone more and watching videos. (Alfred, Sprinter Boy, Harvard)

Alfred's desire to do well academically whilst at the same time to hang out with his peers clearly caused him some difficulty. The American students had a much stronger sense of Black identity. Far more of the British students rejected their Black identity in their expressed choice of music, food, clothes, and their preferred ethnicity of girlfriends. Erick is one of the few students who appeared to have largely rejected his racial identity.

I don't have many posters up. Everybody has standard icons like Bob Marley, Jimmy Hendricks, Mohammed Ali, Martin Luther King and Malcolm X on their walls, I don't though. There's nothing on my wall that's Black and I don't speak patios. My mum was brought up in a household that spoke proper English. It was an educated family. I think that if you're in England you ought to speak proper English. (Erick, Marathon Boy, Oxford)

Even when they wore something that was largely associated with Black culture, some of the UK students were ready to deny its association with Black culture. One student was wearing plaits in his hair and a cap when he was interviewed for this study, but when I pointed this out to him, he replied *'I dress neutrally, apart from the hair, hat and band, I dress neutrally. I walk around with bangles on, how many Black guys do you know who do that?'* And a student from Oxford University who admitted to preferring Caribbean food, hastily added: *'but that doesn't mean I don't enjoy an English roast'*. Yet these students showed no tension over rejecting some aspects of Black identity.

Discovering and coming to terms with their racial identity was another matter. Wilton, for example, who was mixed race, distinctly remembers having to be taught about race by his parents.

I would have preferred to have kept my innocence but I now realise that there is no way I could function in the world, so I did have to think about it. My parents told me that I am generally considered to be Black, so that is usually how I think of myself. In a lot of ways it is something that I've tried to balance out daily in my life. (Wilton, Sprinter Boy, Harvard)

Wilton had a good deal of support from his parents, who made a concerted effort to help him stake out an identity which they felt would be more suitable for him in a White dominated society. On the other hand, Sam, also with mixed heritage, found the process of formulating his racial identity difficult. It took him longer to shape his identity, which was strongly influenced by the wider society's perception. This eventually led to feelings of alienation. Neil describes how he felt whilst staking out his racial identity at school:

> I remember when I had a wakening to racial consciousness, I became sensitive to race issues. I spoke openly about it in grades 7 and 8. Once I brought a book to school which was about how to teach your kids not to be racist. I was revolutionary during my racial awareness years; I was staking out my identity, challenging students and teachers. Actually being provocative, I wrote this satirical essay called 'what if everyone woke up Black one day'. It was turning the stereotype on its head; it was saying 'you White guys don't know Black people; you just believe what you see on television... ghettos, super stars, rappers'. One of the parents who wasn't happy about my essay telephoned the Head and complained about it...

> I lived in a wealthy, upper middle-class area. The neighbours socialise with each other but not with us, being the only Blacks in the area. If there was a school connection, then I would visit their home, that's it. I was treated differently, but I wanted to fit in when I was younger. My parents wanted me to identify with White people more, but as I got older I wanted to identify with my Black side. With White people, I felt I was on display; I had to conduct myself in a certain way. With Blacks, it was easier going and more fun; we could talk about similar experiences. On the other hand, it was hard for me to bridge the gap with some Blacks as I was not into popular culture, I wasn't against it, just not interested, but it's very important for young kids. (Neil, Sprinter Boy, Harvard)

Neil's account draws attention not only to the issues of identity because of being part of two cultures but also to issues around social class. Being from an upper middle-class background, he had not acquired all the same tastes as his peers from lower-class backgrounds and this created some tensions. Erick noted how he differed from the Black boys in his primary school because he was the only one from a middle-class background. He believes this accounted for the difference in such things as their preferences in music. He was inclined to listen mainly to classical music and although he did listen to music such as R&B, he did not appreciate it as much.

Concluding remarks

Racism was perceived to be a major part of the boys' school experience irrespective of social class, country, university attended or educational heritage. With only two exceptions, all experienced some form of racism at school, encountering verbal and, to a lesser extent, physical abuse. There was also evidence of much teacher racism. Teachers displayed racist behaviour and attitudes, meted out differential treatment and held low expectations of their Black pupils. Institutional racism also characterised many of the schools, particularly those which were predominantly White. Whilst some schools were intolerant of pupils behaving in racist ways, others left the boys to find their own way of coping with it – ways which were sometimes considered unacceptable by the school authorities.

The incessant racism in their daily lives and their quest to establish their personal identities combined to put the students in this study under constant stress. It affected their emotional and psychological wellbeing but the tensions they were experiencing were seldom recognised by their schools or by society.

Most of the boys struggled through difficult processes, but a few appeared to have rejected their racial identity outright. Tensions arose between their endeavours to achieve academically and their desire to fit in with their peers, sometimes spilling over and manifesting itself in non-conformist behaviour at school.

There was however, a significant difference between the experiences of the students from the UK and the USA, possibly because the percentage of Black people is much higher in the USA, and they have been settled there for longer. So Americans thus have a clear sense of their position in society. Whereas the Black British, who have mostly been in the UK for only two or three generations, are still going through the process of staking out their position in society. Consequently, it was the British boys who were more likely to reject their racial identity, although this was true of only a few of them.

5

Boys with attitude

M any of the theories which seek to explain the underachievement of
Black boys place the spotlight on Black boys themselves. Whilst
Bleach (2000) takes a gender perspective, blaming the laddish culture
of boys that disparage academic work, Majors (2001), Sewell (1997) and Kreisberg (1992) take a race perspective. They attribute the non-conformist behaviour of Black boys at school to a Black male subculture which has
developed partly as a survival strategy in White dominated society. These
various theories, many of them intertwined, offer a cocktail of gender and
race based explanations for the behaviour of Black boys and their disengagement. It might be assumed that successful Black students differ from the
many who underachieve by being conformist and pro-education. This chapter seeks to determine whether this is true.

Attitudes towards school

Several of the students had exhibited characteristics similar to the students in
Mac an Ghaill's study (1988) who developed a specific mode of resistance
within accommodation by taking a pro-education but anti-school perspective. Whilst these boys conformed to demands made of them: working in
class, completing assignments, doing homework and preparing for examinations, they did not always conform to the school's social demands. So they
were often punished. This study found that over a third of these boys had had
negative attitudes towards school.

Jakim: a vignette

In an inner city area of London Jakim, a Marathon Boy who attended Wolverhampton University, was brought up in a single parent family. He vividly describes his attitude towards school.

Waking up in the morning and having to go to school was like a nightmare; I hated school. I use to bunk off from school on a regular basis, sometimes for months at a time. It got to the point where I simply refused to go to school, so my mum took me out of school and taught me at home for most of year 7 and year 8. My mum spent two years trying to get me back into school. When I did eventually go back, I was placed in a lower set. The lessons were so easy that sometimes I felt I knew more than the teachers. I wanted to move up into a higher class because I found the work too easy but they wouldn't let me, so I stopped going to school again.

... In secondary school I was rebellious. I rebelled against more or less everything, even doing coursework; I questioned why we had to do it. I had a different ideology about school; I had my own goal, and that had nothing to do with studying.

... I took 12 GCSEs but only passed one, but then I deliberately didn't do any revision to spite some of my teachers, plus I slept through my exams.

Jakim looks back now on his wasted years with regret. But immediately after leaving school he turned himself around, inspired by one of his lecturers at college. This time he re-engaged with education and resat his GCSEs, passed, went on to pass A-levels and is now studying a degree in English. He intends to do his PhD and become an English lecturer.

Jakim was undoubtedly disengaged from education at school. His disaffection was manifested in his self exclusion from school for long periods of time and the way he failed his GCSE exams. Other students said things like 'School was horrible' and 'I didn't like school', but surprisingly only one student disliked school because of his inherent dislike of learning. Sam told me:

I didn't want to go to school or enjoyed it; I was more into football rather than academic work. I wanted to be a footballer. I didn't like the education side of school but I enjoyed the social side. I always knew at the back of my mind though that education is necessary, but I never enjoyed it. (Sam, Relay boy, Wolverhampton)

Sam's feelings about school were atypical. The boys were more likely to say that they 'didn't see the point to it' [school] or that 'I went to school but I had no idea what it was for'. They complained about finding certain lessons irrelevant, and being taught about 'things I didn't feel there was any real use for'. Some were troubled by the teaching style of certain teachers. Julieus describes the difference between two teachers' teaching styles.

We had two teachers for English. The one teacher was alright, I was attentive and everything for her lessons, but the other teacher's lessons were so boring, he put me to sleep every time. His voice was so boring, but it wasn't just his voice because I could put up with that, but all he would do in the lesson was just read from the book. When he became ill and we had another teacher, I started to enjoy the lesson as he [the new teacher] made the lessons fun; he made it more interactive. (Julieus, Marathon Boy, Wolverhampton)

Jakim complained about being placed in a set which was below his ability. He felt he was not being mentally stretched and began to think he knew more than his teachers. He was not the only boy who had no intellectual challenge in class, and this often led them to be disruptive. Some distinctly remember being '*miles ahead of the kids in my classes*' and ending up '*messing about*' and getting into trouble because they finished their work well before their classmates. Vincent's account was typical:

> I use to do my work and then started doing other things. My teachers used to say I was distracting others from doing their work. I didn't mean to distract others, but there was nothing else for me to do. I use to do my work quickly to get it out of the way. Others use to follow me, but the difference was I never did anything quickly without understanding it, whereas some of my friends didn't understand the work. Sometimes, I would play truant; it didn't really matter though because if you were in the clever set, then you already knew the work, so you didn't really need to go to the lessons. (Vincent, Relay Boy, Oxford)

Vincent was not the only student to play truant because he was bored in lessons. Bill, a Marathon Boy from Oxford University who enjoyed school overall, became disengaged whenever he got bored. He talked about a time when he was living with his aunt whilst his mum went back to Ghana to bury her mother, and how during that time he would '*sneak out of school, go back to the house and read a book*'. He confessed that '*every now and then I'd play truant and then forge a letter from my mum to say I had a cold*'. But he only behaved like this when he was '*bored at school*' and felt he was learning nothing.

The most common reason for becoming disengaged with school was conflict with teachers. Nearly a quarter of the students, half of them Marathon Boys, had ongoing conflicts with their teachers. In several cases the conflict arose because they considered the lessons irrelevant or disliked the way they were taught. Wilton, for example, confessed:

> I had a very stubborn sense of what was not worth putting my effort into. There were times when I would argue with the teacher about an assignment because I thought it was a silly assignment; I couldn't see the point. My teachers tended not to like that, especially coming from a second or third grader, as if it really was not my place to be telling the teacher what to teach and what not to teach, but I would do so nonetheless. Even when the teachers did try to explain it to me, it got to the point where once I made up my mind about the work, their explanation would be too late;

I wasn't going to change my mind. Sometimes the whole experience made me become very frustrated and I would end up saying rude things to the teachers; that got me into lots of trouble. (Wilton, Sprinter Boy, Harvard)

Some of the boys were rude to teachers but others, like Henroy, became disruptive in class.

At primary school I use to be very bubbly and happy and then I became very depressed and started having anxiety problems. I was so dissatisfied with school. I didn't like (and still don't like) taking people's word, including teachers, I needed to know for myself. I didn't like being lectured; I was always inclined to say 'yes but, yes but, yes but', and that's how I learned best. I could ruin a class, with just me and the teacher debating. I had a passion for arguing on anything but the school didn't allow me to talk enough, so I created havoc. There was so much sitting and listening and everything was one way, them talking; I hated that. I enjoyed the classes where the teachers were willing to engage with me. I suppose I refused to be shaped into being a particular type of pupil. Then one day something just crashed in me and I became a bitter little kid. I ended up having to go to a psychotherapist. (Henroy, Sprinter Boy, Oxford)

Their struggle for control over their own lives and their resistance to the domination of the school system affected the students in different ways: psychologically for some like Henroy and academically for others like Jestin.

In junior school, the teachers were the main reason why I didn't like school. I didn't like my primary school teachers, so I always got into trouble. They didn't like me; it was personal. I was never rebellious; in fact I was a quiet child. During my last year at primary school my parents moved me to another school. Things got much better and my work significantly improved. It's like everything picked up from there. (Jestin, Marathon Boy, Wolverhampton)

Jestin felt that his primary school teachers disliked him, so even though he was not rebellious by nature, he found himself in conflict with teachers. However, not all the students claimed to be the innocent party in such conflicts.

I got detentions for being insolent and for taking the mick out of teachers. I would never pick on other pupils; it was always directed at the teachers. Once I had just finished reading a report which revealed that the average qualifications of teachers to get into teachers' training courses, had declined, so I raised my hand and said 'have you read this article? What do you think? Do you fall into this category?' That got me a detention. I never got detention for fighting or bullying or anything like that, it was mainly for being insolent and occasionally for not doing my homework. (Bill, Marathon Boy, Oxford)

Conflicts of this nature could lead to detentions or even suspension. Nearly half the boys who were given detentions got them because of conflict with a teacher, whether '*arguing with the teachers*', '*back chatting the teachers*', or '*having a go at a teacher*'. Fabian had ongoing conflicts with his teachers and regularly received detentions all through year 7 and even more so throughout year 8. Once he was given three detentions in one lesson and on another occasion he was suspended for having a dispute with the Headteacher, which ended with her sending him home to '*cool down for a couple of days*'.

The laddish culture

The students observed that boys and girls had different attitudes towards schoolwork: '*the girls were like, for education*'; '*the girls worked harder and smarter, they know what to do, what it is to make them wiser*'; '*the girls put a high premium on education*'; and '*it was all right for them to be smart in the classroom, they were very proud of getting A grades*'. But it was unacceptable for the boys to be seen to be working hard at school. Indeed, many of them said they were at risk of being ostracised if they did:

> In middle school, if you were smart you were kind of an outcast. You were looked down on for focusing on school. You can be smart but you can't devote all your time to school. If I say I had to study when they wanted to say, go to a basket ball match, they'd call me a punk – i.e. a homosexual (Trevor, Marathon Boy, Central Florida)

The laddish culture strongly influenced the schooling of many of the boys. But only one student took the view that working hard would be considered 'acting White'. There was, however, much evidence of the influence of the laddish culture and the tension it created for those wishing to conform with their peers while wishing to achieve academically. This was particularly true for the Marathon Boys and Relay Boys.

The pro-education boys were labelled '*swots*', '*kenos*', and '*teacher's pet*', and some were the butt of jokes. Remarks like these were typical:

> It definitely wasn't good to be doing well, especially if you were a boy; it wasn't good. (Henroy, Sprinter Boy, Oxford)

> It was OK to get good grades, providing you were cool at the same time, otherwise you would be considered a boffin. I wouldn't hang around with boffins. (Jakim, Marathon Boy, Wolverhampton)

> They called them nerds, teacher's pet or smarty pants. They didn't call me that, otherwise I'd beat them up. (Rob, Marathon Boy, Central Florida)

> It was not cool to be in the hard working group. They were known as geeks. The goodies weren't involved in socialising or playing sports. (Synesius, Sprinter Boy, Oxford)

Henroy, a Sprinter Boy from Oxford University, summed up the classic trouble makers who made his life difficult and labelled him a '*keeno*'. These pupils thought they were '*cool*' and that '*work wasn't fun*'. Henroy described them as the '*who gives a damn, I don't care type of kids*'.

Peer pressure could be indirect, subtly colouring the general attitudes, priorities, interests and values of peers. The boys described the attitudes of their close friends thus:

> There were twelve of us in my close circle of friends. Most of them just messed about. (Simon, Sprinter Boy, Wolverhampton)

> I had, like, a bunch of friends, the ones who didn't make it, they didn't really care. They'd go to school, sometimes fall asleep, and sometimes they didn't even show up for school, or when they did, they dress with: the jewellery, the shorts, the pants, the hat, and everything to match, just to show off. They didn't do their work, they weren't interested in education, they just wanted to be seen by females. (Albert, Sprinter Boy, Central Florida)

> My friends had no interest in school. Out of my ten close friends, only three got their GCSEs. (Delroy, Marathon Boy, Oxford)

> My friends were tough and popular and most did not have a positive attitude towards school. Quite a few of them dropped out of high school. (Ray, Relay Boy, Central Florida)

Some students were put under pressure by their classmates to engage in socially unacceptable activities in school such as drinking alcohol, smoking and '*selling drugs and doing illegal stuff*', whilst others simply took a complacent attitude towards school. But as Jestin reveals, some of the boys were influenced by their peers.

> I noticed the rapid decline in the Black boys' performance as we went through our secondary school. Attendance started to drop back. It particularly became noticeable in the third year. Up until that time some of my friends were good athletes and good students but then third year came, and they didn't have any focus on what they wanted to do when they left school. Some started to become drug dealers, gang members etc. In my third year I got caught up in all that, i.e. the 'I can't be bothered attitude'. I lost focus (Jestin, Marathon Boy, Wolverhampton)

Black boys behaving badly

Nearly half the students in this study could be deemed to have behaved badly at school. Whilst only a third of the Sprinter Boys considered themselves to be rebels, two thirds of them had at some time been suspended from school. Over half the Relay Boys considered themselves to have been rebels during their school years, and most had had suspensions. Interestingly, rebels and conformists alike were subjected to suspensions. The Marathon Boys had similar behavioural patterns to the Relay Boys, but most of them thought they had been rebellious, although less than half had been suspended. However, all except one had detentions, mostly multiple detentions.

Michael: a vignette

Michael, a Marathon Boy from Wolverhampton University, comes from a single parent, lower-class background and has one sibling, an older sister who is at university. He vividly describes his behaviour during his childhood.

> I was bad! I was just a bad, bad, bad kid! My mum could tell you stories of how bad I was. I was such an embarrassment to her; I was horrible! When I was really young I use to look like a girl because I had long hair and wore cane-rows. There was this one time, during my primary school years, I was sitting down on the train and this woman was looking at me and saying things like 'isn't she cute'. My mum looked at her and smiled but I looked on the woman and spat on her. On several occasions when I used to go out with my mum I would just throw myself down in the middle of the street and either refused to move or I would be kicking my mum or grabbing things and throwing them around the store. Once this Greek man saw me kick my mum really hard and he came up to me and told me I shouldn't be doing that, so I started fighting him. When I got home I got a beating.

> I had an uncle who was bad. He left home when he was 15; he has nine kids. Everyone thought I was going to be like him just because I had his temper. I got on with this uncle, I could relate to him; he didn't encourage me or anything though. I wanted to be like him in some ways, but not entirely like him. He was my role model for a while.

> ... My primary school was rubbish. That was the worst start to education anybody could have. In my secondary school I was in a class they called the 'Wall Class' and we were known as the 'Wall Boys'. It was the Black boys' class, no teacher liked teaching us. We just messed about. School was just somewhere you had to go. I was told to go to school, that's the way it is. I wasn't really bothered about getting an education. I didn't know what I wanted to do as a career. They did a lot of career advice but I didn't know what I wanted to do.

> ... In primary school everyone followed me; I was like the ringleader. Everyone wanted to be like Michael. It used to get to my head sometimes. I wasn't interested in education; I was more interested in my popularity. In secondary school, I was in the lower class. I don't understand why they do sets, it didn't give you a lot of confidence knowing that you were in the bottom set. Because we were in the bottom set we acted tough, because that was the way we got respect from the other kids. Most of my friends were smart, they could have done it [got their GCSEs] but we just didn't focus.

...I had a short temper. If anyone upset me I was quick to open up my mouth without thinking about what I was saying. I was too outspoken. Throughout my school years I was rebellious. I broke most of the school rules. There's no point in rebelling when you go for a job. They will expect you to have a certain haircut and that's the way it is. I know that now! I was never permanently excluded, but I was suspended for things like fighting and being cheeky to the teacher. I use to get detention after detention after detention. It was good though because there was nothing to do in detention sessions so I use to get my homework done.

My only sister, Carol, she was perfect; she got straight As; she's now at university. She used to just work. In my GCSE mocks I got just grade Ds, Es and Fs. When mum used to go to my sister's Parents Evenings, it was just praises, but when she went to mine, which was very intense, she'd come back very upset. There was such a big contrast between us.

Michael was caught up in a vicious circle of misbehaviour, poor performance, low self esteem as a learner, misbehaviour ... round and round. The issue of self esteem at school applied to about quarter of the students. Michael's self esteem was eroded by finding himself placed in the bottom stream, his damaged pride, the vicious circle of misbehaviour, punishment and his poor performance. Michael is a classic example of a boy who assumed a 'cool pose' (Majors and Billson, 1992) as a strategy to keep up his general self esteem amidst his failing grades. Along with other Black boys in his class who had similar abilities, Michael was in danger of dropping out of the educational system altogether (Kerckhoff, 1977 and Kerckhoff *et al*, 2001).

Both Fabian and Lester were ringleaders at school. Fabian, a Relay Boy from Wolverhampton University, was part of a 25 member crew with its own sub-culture. They were the in group, and they more or less ruled the playground. As the cool guys, whatever they wanted from other pupils, they got. Lester, the leader of the Cool Black Boys crew in his school describes his posse:

They were very big on pride and respect, you can't disrespect them. That's some-thing that really upsets them; they want to be respected in everything that they do. Respect to them is not telling them what they can and cannot do. They felt that if they want something, that's what they're gonna get. I'm pretty much like that. What-ever was cool at the time, these boys would take it to the next level. (Lester, Mara-thon Boy, Central Florida)

Michael was one of the Wall Boys, a class of Black boys on whom the school had more or less given up. He was also surrounded by a wider group of Black boys in the school who were constantly in trouble. Michael said that in his school '*Black boys got into trouble more; you'd walk into the detention room and it was Black.*

Detentions were commonplace for the majority of the students in this study.

> I was a clown and a trouble-maker. The teachers didn't really have much patience with me cos my sister and my cousins who are like three years older than me, went to the same school, and because they had a bad name, when I came the teachers were like 'haah!', as if to say, yeah, 'another one of them'. I kinda just lived up to that expectation and gave them cause to beat me up. I got detention for just being a clown, or talking or messing with the girls and whatever, for being easily distracted, you know, hormones and all of that'. (Fabian, Relay Boy, Wolverhampton)

The boys described various situations that earned them detention: '*doing boyish things like throwing paper around*', '*messing around*', '*being a clown, fighting, not doing work in class or not doing homework*'. One student said, '*I got hundreds of detentions for not doing my work and for turning up late*'. Others admitted to '*not always being on the right side of the rules, to be fair*', being a '*terror*' and '*causing all sorts of trouble*'.

These students were also frequently suspended from school because of their behaviour, some of them several times over. Take Fabian for example:

> I got suspended many times. One time I gave a boy concussion, another time I threaten a teacher verbally, then I kinda picked something up in anger; another time I had another fight. Another was with the Headteacher, I told her that she was wrong and she didn't like to hear that, so she sent me home and told me to cool down for a couple of days. (Fabian, Relay Boy, Wolverhampton)

Lester confessed with some embarrassment to being suspended almost once per month during one spell for things like having too many detentions, arriving late to classes and fighting. Fighting was the most common reason for suspension. Every one of the boys in this study who had been suspended had been suspended for fighting at least once. Jakim confessed to an exceptionally serious incident for which he was suspended:

> I use to get bullied so I would fight back, cos the teachers wouldn't do anything about the bullying. I use to pick up chairs and throw them at them; I had a hot temper. Once I put a dinner knife to one of the bullies who was bullying my friend. I got suspended for five days. (Jakim, Marathon Boy, Wolverhampton)

The way Jakim dealt with being bullied and with his teacher's non-responsiveness to his complaints may appear to be exceptional, but a theme through much of the data was how determinedly the students stood up for themselves. Instead of 'learning helplessness, giving up or stopping going to school altogether' when their complaints were not taken seriously (Majors, 2002), they were prepared to tackle the perpetrators themselves.

55

Concluding remarks

The non-conformist attitudes and behaviour associated with the laddish culture (Bleach, 2000) and Black male subculture (Majors, 2001, Sewell, 1997) was indisputably evident during the schooling of many of the boys in this study. Most of them displayed some non-conformist behaviour: negative attitudes towards school, conflicts with teachers and all the detentions and suspensions they were given. Whilst some simply disliked school, others wanted school to be academically challenging and wished for acceptance in White society.

Only a few boys used 'cool pose' as a survival strategy. Most employed more constructive alternatives at school (discussed in Part Three). However, there was much evidence to support Kreisberg's theory that schools are sites of on-going conflict and struggle for control. Black boys' resistance to domination took various forms: truancy, challenging the teachers' teaching style, direct conflict with teachers and with other pupils and bringing so many detentions and suspensions on their own heads.

Many of the boys associated with peers who devalued education and assigned feminine characteristics to anyone who was pro-school. They were subject to being labelled and becoming the target of jokes. Some found it difficult to keep in with their peers whilst striving to achieve academically.

This study has found that a good many of these successful students had in fact been anti-school. They were non-compliant and resisted teachers' authority; some even fought or truanted from school. So how then did they achieve academic success? The answer is explored in Part Three of this book.

PART THREE
UNRAVELLING THE FACTORS THAT GENERATE SUCCESS

6

How parents steer their sons towards educational success

Chapter 3 revealed much evidence that some of the students' parents did not live up to the traditional model of 'good parent' in the educational context. Many did not attend Parents Evening and their level of direct involvement in co-educating their sons at home dwindled as their sons got older – if indeed it ever began. And yet all the young Black males in this study considered their parents to have greatly contributed to their educational success. Whilst there is a general agreement in the literature about the importance of parental influence on the educational attainment of children (Desforges and Aboucharr, 2003) and, to a lesser extent, Black children (Gillborn and Gipps, 1996; Tomlinson 1983b), little research has been carried out into the nature of Black parental involvement and still less on the parents of educationally successful Black boys. This chapter examines the nature of parental involvement in the lives of the Black boys in this study.

The model of Black parents' involvement

Their parents employed various strategies to aid the boys' educational achievement. The perceptions of the students in this study of how their parents gave them effective educational support has built up a model of Black Parent Involvement (see Figure 6.1). The model distinguishes between internal and external parental support mechanisms. The former are the ways in which parents supported their sons at home, whilst the latter represents ways in which parents supported their sons outside the home. Each of the eight sub-themes of the model is discussed.

Figure 6.1: The Black parent involvement model

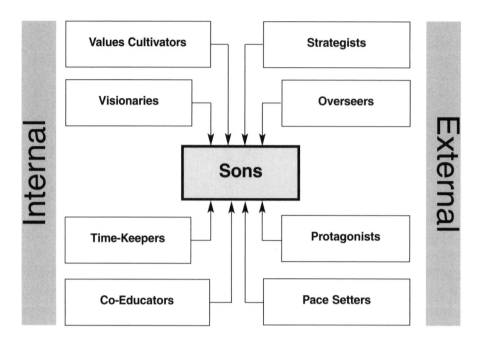

Internal support mechanisms

Values cultivators: parents instilling the value of education

Over three-quarter of the students said that their parents instilled in them the value of education, although not all gave them practical help. Being immersed in pro-education values is clearly a key to success. This is true irrespective of social class, as the quotes from students from lower social classes affirm:

> They (my parents) placed a premium on education. (Alvin, Sprinter Boy, Harvard)

> My parents always stressed the importance of education as being the top priority. (Errol, Marathon Boy, Central Florida)

Some of the subtle ways in which parents instilled such values into their sons can be gleaned from Erick's account.

> I would notice when I went to my friend's house there weren't many books around and if there was one around, they would be expected to tidy up and put it away. However my mum was different; if my room was messy because there were books on the floor, it didn't really matter because they were books, so she didn't count them as mess. (Erick, Marathon Boy, Oxford)

Erick is amongst the majority of the students in this study whose parents were not educated to degree level. Only one third of the students had parents who had a university degree and only a few could boast that their grandparents had been to university. Parents from lower social class backgrounds tended to view education as being the way out of their social and economic sphere:

> She always told me that education is important. Over here if you're Black and you have no education it is very difficult. My mum pushed me. (Brian, Marathon Boy, Central Florida)

Certain comments cropped up frequently: '*my dad didn't want me to end up like him*', '*my parents always told me they wanted me to do better than them*', and '*my parents' life was hard, so they tried to give me a good start in life*'.

The parents' approach to education took different forms. The parents of Sprinter Boys – all of whom were from middle-class backgrounds – were far more likely to have high expectations of their sons. Having themselves achieved academic credentials, they expected their sons to do the same.

> To say that my parents were demanding sounds harsh, but I can't think of another word. They knew if I tried hard I could get A's in my classes. Even though B's are not a bad grade, they would not let me settle with that. (Wilton, Sprinter Boy, Harvard)

High expectations were found equally in two parent and single parent households. Johnson *et al*'s (1988) study into children from lower social backgrounds headed by mothers found that their academic success was not impeded and concluded that 'it is not the number of parents but the level of parental expectations regarding academic achievement that is the determining factor in the educational success of educationally achievement of African-American youth'.

Many students claimed that their parents pushed them, some in a cajoling manner and others more forcibly:

> Even when our school deteriorated, we (he and his siblings included) still got our grades; but that wasn't down to the schools, it was down to our parents busting our arse. (Fabian, Relay Boy, Wolverhampton)

> My mum pushed me. I don't approve of how she went about it; she forced me to study. I didn't enjoy studying when I was younger, but she really, really pushed me. She had a one track mind; it was centred on gaining an education. (Bobzy, Relay Boy, Central Florida)

One student alleged that it was not just him his parents pushed but the school too, because '*they put pressure on my school to give me homework*'.

Visionaries: parents keeping their sons focused

Tomlinson (1983a) identified parents' encouragement as key to Black academic success and this was confirmed by Rhamie and Hallam (2002). Over half the respondents in this study said that their parents were visionary and encouraging. Several confessed that at times when they felt like giving up their parents kept them on track.

> I've had very trying times, horrible times, it can be very stressful, very lonely; times when I've just wanted to quit but my mother gave me a reason to fight, she encouraged me : 'you can do it, look how far you've come, keep on going'. Sometimes that's what I needed and she feeds me well!. (Hugh, Sprinter Boy, Oxford)

Students described their parents as '*the number one main driver*'; as being the one '*in the passenger seat helping me out*'; as being '*my backbone*'; and as the person who had '*pushed me into the right direction*'. Even Trevor had vivid memories of his mother's encouraging attitude, even though she spent most of his school years in prison.

> Mum had it rough, but she always encouraged me; she has never at any point stopped encouraging me even when she was in prison. She still tells me to go to bed at 8 o'clock (laughs). (Trevor, Marathon Boy, Central Florida)

Nearly half the students were from households headed up by their mothers, yet they succeeded academically. Households headed by women survive in the Black community because of the cultural tradition and the extended family, and also the support of the church community, to which many parents, particularly those from the USA, belonged.

The students valued the input to their education made by their parents generally – although not always at the time. Alvin's comment is:

> The problem is you don't see the fruits of education until you get to the end of high school and get into college. That's why your parents have to have a vision for you. My parents use to say, 'I know you can't understand this but you have to trust me'. (Alvin, Sprinter Boy, Harvard)

Time keepers: parents managing their son's time

Conventional wisdom dictates that homework has the power to foster discipline, responsibility and initiative (McDermott, 1984). Some studies support the benefit of homework (Black, 1996; Huntsinger, 1999) while others challenge it (Corno, 1996; Cooper *et al*, 1998). Despite the longstanding debate, homework has become ingrained into the fabric of schooling in both the UK and USA. The commitment of many of the parents to their son's education was demonstrated in their management of their time at home, the main way in which they supported them:

> The emphasis of my parents' involvement in my education was in me putting in the time in my work, rather than helping me directly as such. They would ensure that I did the work. During my early years at school, between the age of 4 and 8, I was behind as a child, so my parents set up a routine for me at home whereby I had to study for two hours every day, Monday to Friday. I started this routine from a young age and continued with it throughout my school years; I got use to it. (Delroy, Marathon Boy, Oxford)

Parents managed their son's time by using playtime and TV as a carrot. They encouraged their children to '*watch the decent programmes on TV like those on the school channel*' and even the news, so they would be '*aware of what was going on*'. One student described watching the news as a privilege: '*I used to be able to watch the 9 o'clock news before I went to bed*'.

Co-educators: parental support in the home

The literature associates strong positive relationships between parental involvement at home and high school achievement (Desforges and Aboucharr, 2003). Most of the parents of the students in this study provided 'professional labour' in the home, a term coined by Reay (2000) to describe the teaching and support parents gave them at home which resembles that given by teachers. Some parents became actively involved in co-educating their sons because they were concerned about a particular aspect of educational provision at the school:

> I wasn't really a disruptive child but I went through a phase when I just got a bit bored at school and mum felt it was because I wasn't being challenged, so she used to take me aside and give me some mental arithmetic to work through. She bought me these timetable tapes which I used to play endlessly. (Erick, Marathon Boy, Oxford)

Others made direct efforts to improve their son's attainment:

> My weakest subject was maths; it would stand out in all my results as I was good at history, good at English, good at everything else except maths. But my father wasn't having it; he didn't want to accept – and neither did I – that I was inherently bad at maths, so he learnt the GCSE maths syllabus just so he could teach me. We spent 40 minutes a day on maths for five years. He just wanted me to get a good GCSE just to prove that I was numerate and then he said I could drop the subject. I got a grade A in my GCSE. (Henroy, Sprinter Boy, Oxford)

Henroy's father was closely involved in educating his son. His determination to prove to the school that nothing was beyond his son's ability to achieve impacted upon Henroy, who was proud about gaining grade A in GCSE maths. Other parents provided support to their sons in less intensive ways, checking their work and requesting that the school give their son extra homework.

A few parents supported their sons at home by engaging home tutors, but only two students from lower social backgrounds had tutoring.

External mechanisms
Strategic moves: choice of school

The premium parents placed on education was reflected in their choice of school. Over a quarter of the students made reference to their parents' careful selection of school – even though choice is limited in the UK and even more restricted in the USA. The boys who lived in middle-class neighbourhoods – half the students in this study – could access schools with high attainment rates. Families who had economic capital were able to purchase houses strategically, selecting areas where the schools were known to provide a good education (Walford 1994). One student observed how much better the school was that he went to after his family moved from a poor Black neighbourhood to a middle-class White neighbourhood.

Parental economic capital also allows for the purchasing of 'elite education' (Walford 1994), but only a quarter of my sample attended private schools. All except two of those who went to private schools had parents who were educated to degree level, two thirds of them in the USA. All the students who went to private schools, except for one English boy, ended up attending the elite Universities of Harvard or Oxford.

Sending their sons to private schools was a real sacrifice for single parents and for parents from lower social backgrounds, like Semore's. He told me that:

> My parents paid the fees for me to go to private school, which was about $12000 a year. I remember my parents saying that it was a lot of money, so we had to make some sacrifices. They would say things like 'as long as you show that you are committed and that you want to do the work, we will make it happen; don't worry about the price tag, we will make it happen'. (Semore, Relay Boy, Harvard)

However, economic constraints meant that private school was not an option for everyone. Most of the students from lower economic backgrounds lived in poverty-stricken communities where educational standards were low, resources scarce and where they were surrounded by environmental, moral and social degradation. Only one English and three American boys who lived in poor neighbourhoods rated their schools as 'average', 'good' or 'very good'. They managed to escape their adverse social environment because their parents got them into schools outside their neighbourhood.

A major objective for parents was getting their sons into the best possible school. But the restrictive school choice policies that are enforced in both countries meant that all many of them could do was find the best school in the neighbourhood.

> The educational standards of the schools in the neighbourhood were rubbish, but the school me and my sister went to were the best schools in the area. You know, you have those tables that come out, well her school was in the top ten and my school was also a good school, that's why my mum choice it. (Michael, Marathon Boy, Wolverhampton)

Michael's mother, like all the UK parents, was amongst the first generation of parents to be able to take advantage of the school choice provided by the UK's Education Reform Act of 1988. Although from a poor background, she capitalised on her cultural capital when deciding on the schools for her children.

Although school choice is even more restrictive in the USA, parents who sent their sons to what may have appeared to be an average school in the neighbourhood nonetheless secured a good education for them because they had access to certain competitively selective programmes such as the accelerated programme for gifted students or magnet programmes, which are tailor-made to help pupils obtain particular skills in subjects like reading and writing.

Some parents, however, did not consider any school in their neighbourhood to be a serious option for their sons.

> The school my mum sent me to was miles away; it took me an hour to get to school. She just wanted to get me out of the area. (Bill, Marathon Boy, Oxford)

Moving their sons out of the neighbourhood seldom came easy. It took a fight – one they were prepared to engage in. David describes the struggles his mother had in getting him into a 'good' school:

> My local comprehensive was the worst school in the area. Everyone went there. There were three schools in the area but my mum didn't want me to go to any of them. She applied for me to go to schools outside the area but we were turned down. My mum appealed. She had to fight to get me into the school that I eventually got into. She even told the Local Authority that if I didn't get into that school, then I was going to stay at home. At that age, although I knew I wanted to go to a good school, but at the same time, the comp was where my mates were going. We all knew the local comp. But when I went to my secondary school, it was such a culture shock. I use to travel about an hour to get there. My hair had to be cut a certain way, I had to dress a certain way; but it was a good school. Of the guys I went to school with, two now work for a bank, one works for the Crown Prosecution Service, I'm doing a degree here [at Oxford], another one is doing a post graduate in law, and those guys were in the bottom tier at school, yet they are doing well. Getting into that school has influenced the outcome of my schooling; if I had gone to the local comp I would not have achieved what I've got now. (David, Marathon Boy, Oxford)

It was not just the system that these parents had to challenge but their sons too. Like David, many boys wanted to go to the local school so they could be with their friends. Some parents are influenced by short term considerations and the feelings of their children at the time (Carroll and Walford, 1997). Many of the children whose parents let them decide what school to go to opt for the one their friends are going to. However, the parents of the boys in this study did not allow their sons to decide: the parents made the choice.

The UK school marketplace has been criticised for its rhetoric of school auto-nomy and parental freedom of choice (Carol and Walford, 1997) when in reality it maintains and reinforces social class and ethnicity divisions and in-equalities (Gewirtz *et al*, 1995). Gewirtz *et al* point out that middle-class parents are the most inclined to manipulate the market and the best able to exploit it to their children's advantage. There is less choice in the USA, but it leads the UK in its policy on school choice, making equity issues a major con-sideration. In both countries, however, many of the parents of the successful boys also exploited the market as far as they could. Not only economic capital but also the cultural capital of families matter. The use of cultural capital in the decoding of schools and interpretation of information in the 'matching' of child to school is a crucial component of choosing and then getting a school place.

Overseers: parents who keep an eagle eye on their sons' schools

The parents of most of the boys attended Parent Evenings and Parent Teacher Association meetings. Two of the American parents participated in the gover-nance of their sons' schools. One describes the advantages this gave:

> They [his parents] were active as trustees in elementary school and, to a lesser extent, in high school. It gave me an advantage in the sense that it made me known to the teachers and it raised their expectations of me. I also became aware of the inner workings of the school and its direction. (Neil, Sprinter Boy, Harvard)

Dillon, the other boy whose parent was a trustee, also derived benefits from his mother's involvement in his school. He claims that his mother developed an excellent relationship with the school and still maintains contact today. Both families were middle-class, a factor aligned to the findings of other studies which indicate that it is the most articulate and knowledgeable parents who are best placed to take up these roles (Crozier, 2000).

Although none of the parents of the English boys were involved in the gover-nance of their son's school, one who had concerns about her son became a classroom assistant at his school so she could keep an eye on him. She did not assist in her son's class, but this UK Marathon Boy who got into Oxford University said that her presence in the school served its purpose of keeping him on the straight and narrow.

Protagonists: parents who challenge their son's school

A quarter of the students observed conflicts between their parents and the school. In nearly two thirds of cases the parents were middle-class and had degrees. Wilton describes his parents' relationship with his school:

> In middle school, my parents would get into conflicts with the school administration whenever they weren't happy about something. I remember this one time when I got disciplined and my parents' felt the punishment was too harsh compared to the punishment they would give to other children. One or other of my parents would go to school, a lot of times it would be my mother because my father was at work. My mother would call the school and complain and then she would talk to my dad about it. Then my dad would call from work, and make it clear to them that he was taking time off from his work to deal with it. It always kind of embarrassed me but at the same time I appreciated it; it made me feel good to know that they were challenging the administration. (Wilton, Sprinter Boy, Harvard)

Interestingly, few of the parents from lower social class backgrounds or who had not been to university challenged their son's school. These parents tend to have a neutral relationship with the school or even a positive one, especially the UK parents. Several students complained about how their parents always sided with the teachers '*even if the teachers were wrong*', because '*they always believed what the teachers said*'. A student said '*Mum had a tendency to take the school's side whenever I got into trouble, even though sometimes they actually lied*'.

An equal number of parents from the USA and the UK had conflicts with their sons' school, all of them middle-class and well educated. The sons of these assured parents all went on to Oxford or Havard. Some of the conflicts were to do with the teachers' attitudes towards the boy's education. One student, for example, said his parents were concerned about his teacher's failure to take an active role in getting him back on the right track when they saw his performance slipping. Another student said his mum was concerned about the low expectation teachers held of him, because '*they said things about my ability which didn't match up with what she knew about me*', so his parents moved him to another school.

Some teachers stereotype Black parents as 'aggressive' and might well have perceived these parents in that light. Tony described the interaction between his mother and his teachers:

> My teachers seemed quite frightened of my mum, to tell you the truth. She would go into school with her notepad and pen ready to take notes of whatever they said [laughs]. They knew they couldn't mess her around. She comes across as quite intelligent. She is an assertive Black woman. Mum came to all the boarding house events. When I did have a serious issue she would dive down to see my House Master. By that time she had become an expert in race relations and so she gave them a few lessons about what was going on. (Tony, Sprinter Boy, Oxford)

And Delaney describes his father's response to the situations he had to address with the school:

> My father was, I guess, more aggressive about it. If something was wrong at school he would get very angry and very loud when addressing the teachers. I know that he really wanted us to succeed; also it is inherent in his nature. He is just very in-your-face, he is always to the point. (Delaney, Marathon Boy, Harvard)

Conflict between the parents and the schools were often connected with race. Neil, a Sprinter Boy who went on to Harvard, said that his father had been concerned about '*racial issues being swept under the carpet*', such as when his music teacher taught them a song with the word 'mammy'. Neil himself did not understand the derogative nature of the word at first, so his father made him research it. He then made a formal written complaint to the school and this elicited an apology from the teacher. But parents' complaints did not always have positive outcomes. Bobzy relates his mother's experience:

> My mum became disillusioned with the experience I had, being Black. There were a series of situations where they (kids in his school) told me to 'get out', 'go back to the ghettos' and made death threats. Neither one of us expected that, I was turned off by the social experience; it was a culture shock to my mum. My mum challenged the school on several occasions. She met with the Head of school, but they told her the problem was with me, that I was socially maladjusted, and it was just a phase I was going through. After that she gave up confronting them. (Bobzy, Relay Boy, Central Florida)

Hugh had a similar response from his parents when he complained about a teacher:

> Teachers win all the time. My parents expressed their concerns. It's sad when you go to the Head and you're not listened to. (Hugh, Sprinter Boy, Oxford)

According to Crozier (2000), middle-class parents have a more comfortable relationship or 'fit' with schools. However, whether this is true for Black middle-class parents is open to question. My study found that it was the Black middle-class parents who were more likely to be in conflict with teachers. They were probably better informed about the educational system and had the social capital to be confident about challenging their sons' schools when they thought it necessary, even if it meant being stereotyped as aggressive.

Pacesetters: parents as role models

Some of the boys were inspired by the achievements of their academically successful parents, which made them realise what was possible:

> Excelling in school was a family value. My parents had a major role in that; they are both professionals. They made pursuing excellence the norm, which they have done so blatantly, maybe a little arrogantly. Being trial-blazers, my parents were sometimes the first Blacks in their field, medical school and in my dad's law firm, so I was brought up to reject any thoughts that society won't let me do things because I'm Black. So in subscribing to my parents' expectations, I worked hard to make sure I got a good education. (Neil, Sprinter Boy, Harvard)

In a few cases, the parents modelled their regard for education by returning to studying themselves.

> They encouraged us to go and get an education. Education is sort of perceived as a way out. My mother spent a lot of time with us whilst my dad was working. Eventually my parents, having taught us that education is the key, started to look at themselves and so decided to go back to school because they did not want to contradict their message. My dad would work when my mother went to school and now they are switching places, because my mom is working and my dad is going to school. (Carver, Relay Boy, Harvard)

These students had been strongly influenced by their families' positive attitudes. Clark's study of family life and school achievement (1983) found that children receive essential 'survival knowledge' for competent classroom role enactment from exposure to 'positive home attitudes and communication encounters'.

The students cited their parents, particularly their fathers, as the principal role model in their lives – far more than sports and music personalities, as the stereotypes would have it. Ross (1998) also found that fathers who lived at home were the most significant role model to their sons. Fathers were looked up to by the boys for fulfilling their traditional roles as the '*provider*' and being the one who '*kept the household together*'. Even fathers who were not actively involved in their education were generally acknowledged for the wider role they played in their sons' lives.

> I used to wait for him to follow him after work. I had a great appreciation for what he did. (Ray, Relay Boy, Central Florida)

The boys' second most popular role model was their mother:

My mother made the greatest impact on me. (Levi, Sprinter Boy, Wolverhampton)

My mother is a prime example of what I aspired to. She did not come from a wealthy background, but she built herself up and passed on the torch to me. (Dillon, Sprinter Boy, Harvard)

The role models the students named were not affected by whether they were Sprinter, Relay or Marathon boys. Those who cited their father as their major role model were from two parent households, whereas most of those who cited their mothers were from single-parent households. This is interesting given that mothers, irrespective of the family structure, were the ones who were most actively involved in the education of their sons.

Conclusion

Given the differences in the culture and traditions of Black people in the two countries, the similarity in the parental involvement is striking. The parents were immersed in a pro-education value system and proactive in exploiting the school market for the benefit of their sons. In the USA, however, parents' involvement in homework declined as their sons got older. They were less likely to attend parents' meetings than their British counterparts and more likely to purchase private education, and to participate in the governance of their son's school. To keep up with economic demands, many of the American parents worked long hours and even had more than one job, so they had greater financial resources to pay for private education but little time to support their children's learning.

It was primarily the parents of Sprinter boys who had conflicts with their son's school and these boys, interestingly, all ended up at Oxford or Harvard. These were the parents who were well informed about the education system and had the right social capital to give them the confidence to challenge the schools when they thought it appropriate. They were undeterred by the possibility of being stereotyped as 'aggressive', being accused of 'intimidating the teachers' or of being on the receiving end of negative teacher attitude towards them (Blair and Bourne, 1998).

Most parents encouraged their sons in their school work and supported them, at least in the earlier years. It was mainly the parents of the Marathon boys, who had little or no educational credentials themselves, who lacked the knowledge or confidence to work with their sons.

Yet even these parents made strategic choices to send their sons to the 'best' school. The 'best' school, however, was framed differently according to their social and economic background. Middle-class parents, mostly the parents of

Sprinter boys and Relay Boys, regarded these as being the high achieving schools in the affluent neighbourhoods in which they could afford to live, or private schools which they could afford to pay for. In the absence of economic capital, the parents of the Marathon Boys drew on their social capital to get their sons into the best school – that is the best they could access in or indeed outside their poorer neighbourhood.

Whilst most of the parents are perceived to be role models to their sons, again there were slight differences in the modelling process. The Sprinter boys and to a lesser extent the Relay Boys, modelled the path their parents had already taken, whereas Marathon Boys modelled their parents' vision of educational success.

Single parents were less likely to send their sons to private school, engage in conflicts with school or help with homework. But having only one parent at home appeared not to undermine their son's academic performance. Their mothers employed compensatory strategies in pursuit of their son's educational success, instilling in them strong educational values and effectively capitalising on the support of the family network and, particularly in the USA, of the church community.

In sum, the kind of parental involvement in education that is recognised by teachers – that is, professional labour at home and being visible at events such as Parents' Evenings or Parent Teacher Association – requires time, resources and knowledge of the subject matter being taught. However, despite the fact that many of the parents in this study did not possess these assets, they were still effective in supporting their son's education with a diverse range of strategies, some traditional and widely accepted and others not. What they had in common was their strongly held educational values. It was their values which underpinned so much of what they said and did, which so enhanced the educational achievement of their sons. In so doing, they made an indirect but invaluable contribution to the upward social mobility of the next generation of the Black community.

The overwhelming majority of the parents of Sprinter boys and Relay boys had themselves been Marathon children whose own parents had not been to university. By fostering their sons' educational success these parents are preventing adverse cultural reproduction, halting the passing down of long-standing disadvantages and inequalities from one generation to the next.

This brings hope for the future. As Marathon and Relay Boys join the race, they pave the way for the emergence of more Sprinter boys in the future. The children of the boys in this study will enter the education market having already possessed, in Bourdieu's terms, quantities of relevant capital bestowed upon them in the process of habitus formation. Their children will be amongst the privileged: they will have learned the appropriate behaviour and be equipped with the dispositions of both manner and thought to ensure their success within the education system.

7

Teachers in schools and community projects

I n both the UK and the USA, teachers have been identified as contributing to Black boys' under-achievement (Osborne, 1997a; Fordham and Ogbu, 1986; DfES, 2003; Ofsted, 1999). Researchers have found evidence of institutional racism and teacher racism (Rampton 1981; Gillborn, 1990; Hopkins, 1997; Sewell, 1997; Blair *et al*, 1998; O'Leary and Betts, 1999; Majors, 2001). However, my study found that although the overwhelming majority of subjects had been on the receiving end of racism, there were also teachers whom the boys singled out for significantly enhancing their educational achievement. Teachers were a major influence in the boys' success. This echoes the findings of McAdoo (1988) and Ross (1998). This chapter explores the enabling role of particular White and Black teachers in schools and community projects, to the boys' success.

Three quarters of the students cited one or more of their teachers as having contributed to their academic achievements, a third of them mentioning only Black teachers. This study identified a model of what these Black boys regarded as 'good teachers', that is, teachers who had been enabling. The data collated from interviews with the students were coded into broad themes and then edited, structured and restructured into emerging themes and sub-themes. The sub-themes form the basis for a model of 'Effective Teachers of Black Boys' (see Figure 7.1).

The model has six main sub-themes, each representing an important characteristic of effective teachers of whatever race or ethnicity, as defined by the boys. A further three sub-themes denoted by the inner dotted circle, are

Figure 7.1: The effective teacher of Black boys

included in the model to highlight the added value many Black teachers bring to the schooling of Black boys. These sub-themes are discussed below.

Teachers who display racial empathy

Bourdieu's theoretical concept of cultural capital provides an explanation for the reproduction of educational inequality (Bourdieu, 1986), where the dominant social class (which in the UK and the USA is White dominated) legitimately reproduces its power and privilege. Consequently not everyone has equal opportunity to succeed since the system is structured to favour one class (or race) over another. However, Black boys, irrespective of their cultural capital, enter the education market at a disadvantage and as unequal players because of their race. Virtually all the boys in my study reported being subjected to racism during their schooling. Almost a quarter articulated what can be deemed institutional racism. There were however, some empathetic White teachers and the boys acknowledged their contribution to their high attainment.

> In private high school, I remember my maths teacher was an old White man; he was great. He told me from my first day 'you're going to have to work twice as hard as the other kids here because the colour of your skin can keep you back here. They're going to be looking at your athletic abilities, so you've got to be serious; you have to really get your priority straight and work hard at this school'. (Semore, Relay Boy, Harvard)

> When I was about 13 and I was in trouble, he called me aside and said 'I'm not going to bullshit you; this is the way the world is ... it's going to be more difficult for you to make it in this world because you are Black. I want you to set your ambitions high; I want you to become Prime Minister'. I thought 'wow, he believes in me! He believes I'm intelligent'. He bolstered my self esteem. (Bill, Marathon Boy, Oxford)

Such empathetic teachers reassured the boys that there was someone in the school who understood the challenges Black boys face in society and also at school. Rather than being colour blind, the teachers recognised the existence of racism in the school and society and its power to reinforce inequality and affect educational outcomes. They were aware that Black boys face structural and institutional discrimination because of their skin colour and gender, and sought to support these students emotionally. They encouraged Black boys to embrace the achievement ideology associated with the dominant cultural capital, even though some resisted certain of its cultural manifestations such as White middle-class speech, dress, musical tastes or interactional styles. In the absence of a school environment in which Black students felt a sense of belonging, the racial empathy and moral support of individual teachers helped to give the boys confidence to navigate their way successfully through the education system.

Teachers who are passionate about teaching

Teachers who expended physical, intellectual and emotional investment in their work motivated the boys to work.

> The classes I enjoyed were those where the teachers were very passionate about their subject, like my English teacher. He just loved teaching English. He really enjoyed having discussions about books. Very often I and some of my classmates would stay after the class and talk about books and novels. (Wilton, Sprinter Boy, Harvard)

> My history teacher had studied at Oxford; she was great; she was the best history teacher I ever had. She got me so interested in history. In the national test, her class got the highest grade in the country. She was phenomenal; I loved her to death. She just had so much feeling behind the teaching. She wanted us to learn the material, but more so, she wanted us to understand the meaning behind the material, so we

> learnt the facts about places which we didn't directly need to learn about, but it helped us so much. (Trevor, Marathon Boy, Central Florida)

The teachers' enthusiasm makes a notable difference to their students' learning. Other studies, such as Leitch, *et al* (2003) and Morgan and Morris (1999) also found that those teachers perceived as the best were enthusiastic about their job. They took a genuine interest in their pupils, engaged emotionally in lessons, and their enthusiasm about their work tended to 'rub off on the kids'. These are teachers who have a 'calling' rather than just a job. But teachers being passionate about their work was not enough to engage Black boys in the educational process – the teachers had also to be able to connect with them, as Trevor's had done, making him feel involved in her lessons.

Teachers who use effective teaching approaches

There was little evidence of antiracism or multiculturalism in the schools attended by these Black boys, so they had almost no opportunity to connect racially with the curriculum, nor was the knowledge base of White pupils broadened to embrace new perspectives. The racialised school environment plus a curriculum which failed to reflect their racial identities and cultural tastes, meant that school presented unwelcomed challenges to Black students.

Giroux (1994) sees multiculturalism as creating tolerance, understanding and acceptance of other ideas and beliefs in different cultures, celebrating commonalities between cultures whilst increasing knowledge of differences and banishing stereotypes. But he criticises it for not going far enough to expose White racism or promote social justice. He argues that the discourse essentialises minority cultures and ignores underlying power structures. Giroux proposes a form of 'insurgent multiculturalism' that would strip White supremacy of its legitimacy and authority. However, most of these students did not even encounter multiculturalism, still less an antiracist pedagogy. Teachers formally assess students, but students also assess their teachers, albeit informally. In their assessment of their teachers' understanding of Black boys and their ability to accommodate classroom discussions about race so these were positive, they found that many White teachers' understanding was poor.

> In my school I was the only Black person. There were some teachers who didn't know how to relate to you. Whenever race issues came up they felt uncomfortable. I always felt in the middle of it all, so I tended to withdraw from the discussion. (Sam, Boy, Wolverhampton)

Teachers are not autonomous workers: the available range of approaches to teaching are negotiated around the broader school culture and structure. Nonetheless, nearly a quarter of the students made positive reference to teachers who had effectively negotiated teaching approaches which motivated them to learn.

> One of my teachers put a lot of effort into trying to make his class interesting; not just interesting for the sake of flashy gimmicks, but by making us think about the subject matter. I had other great teachers: they provided me with opportunities to find new challenges and to challenge myself. I feel my English teacher gave me complicated things to do; it really gave me the chance to see how far I could go. One of the things that I really liked about one particular teacher was that instead of returning my work with comments on the paper, he would meet with us and discuss our essays over breakfast. We felt like he had a personal investment in every student. (Wilton, Sprinter Boy, Harvard)

Effective teachers take into account the learning styles of their pupils. Boys' concentration spans are generally lower than girls' (Lightfoot, 1997) and their learning styles also differ – boys' main learning style is experimental (Hinds, 1995). The Black boys tended to learn more in classes where the teachers made their lessons *'fun'* and *'interactive'*, where the teacher *'challenged me'*, *'took into account my personal interest'*, was *'unconventional'* and *'took into account our personalities'*. Such teachers contrasted with those whom the students claimed *'don't pay much attention to Black boys'*, *'favoured Whites over Blacks – and it was obvious'*, *'overlooked them [Black boys] for playing certain roles in school plays or receiving awards'* which they believed they justly deserved.

Thus Black boys benefited from lessons that were fun and interactive, that helped keep them engaged and prevented them from being distracted by the negative aspects of the school's ethos. Blair *et al* (1998) criticise schools for failing to create environments in which the Black students are accepted for who they are and can feel a sense of belonging. They argue that in order to accept and respect students' identities, it is necessary to know and understand them. And it was the personal interest shown by a teacher that made all the difference. Effective teachers of Back boys recognised the differing degrees of dominant cultural capital each possessed – the values, beliefs, norms, attitudes and experiences – and adjusted their teaching to foster their students' learning.

Teachers who were non-judgemental
Nearly half the students said they had had teachers who behaved in racist ways at some time – usually manifested in covert ways such as low

expectations. The low expectations of Black boys held by teachers has been found in much research (Blair *et al,* 1998; Ofsted, 1999; DfES, 2003). However, I found that some of the teachers had expected much of their Black pupils. Hugh compared the teachers he perceived to be the 'good' and the 'bad':

> The bad teachers were not necessarily bad because they didn't know their subjects; the distinguishing factors of the good teachers were in their expectations of you; they made you excited about their subjects, they didn't look at your colour, they just looked at what you're producing and said 'here's someone who's got potential... let's push him. They were academic mentors, that's what you need. (Hugh, Sprinter Boy, Oxford)

Hugh confirms that a teacher's expectations of Black boys was a key factor which he, and many students in this study took into account when assessing their teachers. Tomlinson (1983a) affirmed Rampton's assertion (1981) that the effective teachers of Black pupils have high expectations of them and this encourages them to strive at school.

Although it is widely believed that Black boys underachieve because of their low self esteem, Spencer's USA study (1991) showed that Black boys have higher self esteem than White children. Spencer identified a difference between Black boys' more general self esteem and their 'student' self esteem which was eroded by the school system. Smith (1997) found that the longer Black boys stayed in school the more their 'student self' was eroded. However, a number of students in my study attributed their educational success partly to the confidence their teachers displayed in them, which actually enhanced their student self esteem and thus contributed to their academic performance.

Teachers who were talent spotters
The boys thought highly of the teachers who spotted their talents. Like the students in Cotton's (1998) and White's (2000) studies, they often rated these as their best teachers.

> A teacher, an old White lady, pulled me aside one day and told me that I have a gift and that she wanted to see if I could hold that gift, so she invited me to take a test – a kind of a IQ test – to get me unto a gifted programme. I passed the test. When someone tells you that you can do it, that you are special, you start to believe in yourself. She contributed to instilling the value of education in me, so when things got tough and I was struggling, I knew I had to stick it out. (Semore, Relay Boy, Harvard)

> I remember to this day my second grade teacher in elementary school, Miss Crouch, she distinguished me early on in the class. She said I was a bright student. I didn't see myself as bright until she mentioned it. She picked me out as a student

78

> who was gifted. I had to take a test, but even though I didn't pass it, she still encouraged me. (Ray, Relay Boy, Central Florida)

There is a fundamental problem in the school system over equity. Schools in both the UK and USA have been criticised for the under-representation of Black pupils in gifted and talented programmes. But certain teachers actively sought to identify gifted and talented Black boys. Whilst intellectual abilities are undoubtedly an asset in the pursuit of high academic attainment, many gifted and talented pupils still underachieve (Ford, 1995). Even a grammar school student who participated in my study failed to achieve the national standards of 5 GCSEs grade A*-C at the end of compulsory school leaving age, attributing his underachievement to the institutional racism that pervaded his school. It wasn't until he left school and enrolled at college that he found a more conducive environment to his learning and obtained the qualifications to move up the educational ladder. As Gillborn (1990) argued, ability and dedication are not in themselves enough for Black boys to achieve highly at school.

Effective teachers spotted not only those who were academically gifted students but what their particular strengths were. Sockett (1993) asserted that techniques of teachings are subservient to a moral end, and Day (2004) argued that teaching should be designed to benefit humankind and that an essential attribute of effective teachers must therefore be perseverance. Seeing beyond the present behavioural challenges of students to identifying their talent was a characteristic which for these students distinguished the good teachers.

> Until my third year I was a terror; I was in detention most of the time causing all sorts of trouble. I felt that the teachers were always picking on me, so my first reaction was always, 'you're always picking on me, you're always picking on me'. Then one day, at the age of 13 or 14 a teacher who saw the leadership qualities in me and the negative way in which I was using it, just sat me down and she said 'do you realise that certain people follow you and your lead in the classroom? Have you thought about the effect that might have on other people in the classroom if you changed?' I sat back and thought about it. I thought 'fair enough, I suppose I could change'. (David, Marathon Boy, Oxford)

> There was a particular teacher who recognised my talents even whilst I kept getting into trouble at school. He challenged me into debating and developed my confidence. (Bill, Marathon Boy, Oxford)

These were students who, in Bourdieu's terms, 'presented challenges' in school. However, both David's and Bill's teachers saw beyond their challenging behaviour and focused on maximising their talents. David's teacher's recognition of his leadership qualities was presented in a way he could relate to and proved to be the turning point in his hitherto rebellious behaviour in school. By focusing on his potential rather than his behaviour, Bill's teacher was able to channel his energies in positive ways and thus boost his confidence.

Teachers who developed good interpersonal relations with Black boys
Studies have shown that Black boys are often the victims of differential treatment and double standards concerning harassment, over-monitoring, discipline, length of punishment, the choice of who is to speak in class, and how they are communicated with (Sewell, 1997). They are often disrespected, talked down to, over-monitored, blamed for things they did not do, and given no chance to tell their side of the story (Watt *et al*, 1999); and are singled out for criticism – even when pupils of different ethnicities are engaged in the same behaviour (Gillborn 1990). Many Black boys dis-identify with academics and this adversely affects their attainment levels (Fordham and Ogbu 1986; Osborne 1997a).

Good interpersonal relationships between teachers and pupils are fundamental to successful teaching and learning. Day (2004) describes such relationships as 'the glue that binds the two together and the binding expression of the teacher's commitment to the student as a person'. Caring about Black boys and showing them respect was frequently cited as a major attribute of the teachers who had encouraged the boys.

As far back as 1985 an HM Inspectorate report in England captured the importance of mutual respect between teacher and pupil: 'it is only where this two-way passage of liking and respect between teachers and pupils exists that the educational development of pupils can genuinely flourish' (HM Inspectorate Report, 1985). Glimpses of good interpersonal relationships and the importance of mutual respect are apparent in the following accounts:

> I had a really good maths teacher, he was White. He was 'real' with us. He was cool; he really wanted us to do well. He'd pull me and my friend aside so many times and say 'come on guys' and encouraged us to go to the after-school classes. The good teachers would actually talk to you not just shout at you like some others. They inspired you to do well. Every teacher that I felt was a good teacher I got good grades in their subjects. (Michael, Marathon Boy, Wolverhampton)

> There was my 7th grade teacher, Susan L; she was amazing; she was great. She came to my basketball games; she was so helpful and was there whenever I

needed her; I loved her to death. Then there was my 8th grade teacher, Mr Ham, he told me 'don't let them damn teachers push you around, if you need any help come get me and I'll kick their ass' [laughs]. If I needed help, he was there; he was like a mentor. He was just so funny; he was the kind of guy you'd hang out with; he was so cool. And then there was my kindergarden teacher, I loved her class; she just made it fun. It was easy to learn from her. I loved her to death. She was one of the biggest influencers of my early childhood. She taught me etiquette, things like how to stand, how to be polite, what to do at church. (Trevor, Marathon Boy, Central Florida)

From an early age, I got the impression that certain teachers didn't have much faith in me. If I didn't like the teacher or get on with them, I didn't do well in the class, but if I had a good teacher I would work, and when I did, I realised that I could do well and this built up my confidence. (Delroy, Marathon Boy, Oxford)

The correlation between the pupil-teacher relationship and the student's motivation, confidence and performance has long been established. The teachers who developed good relationships with these Black boys did so by various means – they took a personal interest in them, encouraged them, were friendly towards them, treated them equally and provided them with opportunities to excel. Kinder *et al* (1996) found that changes in teacher-pupil relationships was one major change Black children wished to see in schools. And Majors (2001) observed that approaches that stimulate and support students learning focus on strategies that promote interpersonal relationships and social justice between teachers and pupils.

Added value: how Black teachers can help Black pupils

In the inner part of the model on page 74 of Effective Teachers of Black Boys is the value added by Black teachers to the schooling of Black boys. A quarter of the students in this study had at some time been taught by a Black teacher and a few in the USA had attended schools which had Black Principals or Administrators. Almost half the students from the USA had been taught by, or had access to, a Black teacher in school – especially the students who went to Central Florida University – but this was true for less than one sixth of the UK students. It may be due partly to America's far larger Black population and partly to its affirmative action policies at the time the boys were at school.

A few of the students who had never had a Black teacher expressed indifference: '*It didn't bother me having Black teachers. Black or White, teachers are just teachers at the end of the day really*'. Most, however, would have welcomed it. But some felt strongly about it: '*I hungered for a Black teacher*'. They felt that Black teachers would have brought a '*different perspective to the lessons'*. Fabian, however, was initially cynical about the efforts made by his female Headteacher to address the under-representation of Black teachers in his school in England:

> During our last year she just brought in a whole heap of Black teachers, well maybe not a whole heap, it was about three or four. The first Black teacher she brought in was Mr Leonard. She might have done this for the right reasons, but it came across as being negative to us, like mere tokenism, because she has always had a negative attitude towards Black people. She had this big cloud over her head as a racist, so it's like she was just trying to prove something, trying to be politically correct. A lot of people thought that was basically the reason, because it was just him, one [the only Black teacher appointed].
>
> At first we were a bit sceptical about him, but then he was so positive. It was good having him around, we could relate a lot more to him. He helped all of us, gave us that entire extra boost. He used to take us out after school; everyone brought their bikes round, and we would go out for an evening. He kept us stimulated. The offer was open to everyone, whoever wanted to come, it wasn't a racial thing, but pre-dominately it was us lot that took up the offer, cos we could all relate. He was more like a mentor than a teacher; he did more than just take classes, he seemed like more of a friend, one of the boys, rather than a teacher. (Fabian, Relay Boy, Wolver-hampton)

Having a Black teacher proved to be so positive that Fabian's cynicism was shortlived. The out of school activities the teacher organised was not typical and neither was Fabian's perception of this teacher being *a friend, one of the boys'*. The effective relationship between Fabian and his teacher was characteristic for many of the boys with their Black teachers.

Racial connectedness

An Interesting theme that ran through these accounts was how the boys related to Black teachers.

> I liked having Black teachers; it was like they were one of my own; I felt very comfortable with them. If I was confused about something, I felt able to ask them. There was no favouritism from them but they would listen. (Brian, Marathon Boy, Central Florida)
>
> It was good having them cos they can relate to you, so if I had a problem, even a personal problem or discrimination problem, I felt I could go to them because they've probably been through it before. I would go to them first rather than to the White Principals to tell them of my problems. (Albert, Sprinter Boy, Central Florida)

The boys had perceived Black teachers as approachable because of their shared experience of being Black in a White dominated society. Their presence had a positive impact on the students; it adds value to the school. Blair *et al* (1998) contended that Black teachers understand the problems the children faced and that they could influence their colleagues and the school. Their presence, they argued, helped ensure that practices in the schools were fair.

According to John (1993) the school, with all its structural arrangements, becomes a site for struggle against racism for Black teachers in much the same way as the community outside the school. John points to various ways in which the racism in society is replicated within the school: in the approaches to curriculum and its content, the attitudes of students, staff and parents, the negative expectations held of Black staff and students – and in the assumption that it is principally the responsibility of Black staff to deal with 'difficult' Black students and 'awkward' Black parents' (John, cited in Channer, 1997 p62).

The identity, culture and experiences of Black teachers help shape their practice and enables them to bring a unique dimension to the classroom. Black students' readiness to relate to these teachers may be linked to their teaching style, which is more likely to be culturally sensitive to them. Studies show that many Black teachers seek to connect classroom content with students' experiences and to encourage them to bring community experiences into the classroom (Ladson-Billings, 1990).

Callender (1997) argued that many Black teachers employ teaching styles that join teachers and pupils into a community of learners. She highlights particular features of such pedagogy such as using African communication patterns of call-response, repetition, signifying and non-verbal communication. Call-response is a major organising characteristic of African communication, so is common to Black people on both sides of the Atlantic. It establishes a collective rapport between teacher and pupils and encourages group participation and the establishment of shared norms. Callender found that many Black teachers used African retained features of non verbal communication and paralinguistic modes and features including their eyes, in addition to the spoken word. These strategies enabled Black children to connect culturally with them and to speak frankly about racist incidents.

Encouragement and motivation

The boys thought that the Black teachers treated all their students well: '*it did not matter who you are; she always encouraged you to succeed.*' But they were noted for giving Black students that extra push to maximise their potential.

> I had a Black teacher, he really pushed us more. He made it clear that the reason he was pushing us was because we were Black and once we got out of this area

out of school, we were not going to be in a group of all Black people, so we have to be able compete and we already had one disadvantage of being Black so he pushed us harder because of that. (Bobzy, Relay Boy, Central Florida)

They taught everyone equally within the classroom, but they did take a particular interest in the Black children; they wanted you to do well. Once when I could have gone astray, a Black teacher pulled me to the side and said, 'you shouldn't really be doing anything like that here because they will jump on you'. I appreciated that. When they see you outside of classes, they always say 'how you doing'. (Dumali, Sprinter Boy, Harvard)

The students observed that Black teachers '*went the extra mile*', they '*gave you a little bit more of a push*', '*they always wanted the best for the Black students*'. Their encouragement was part of a wider context of positive interpersonal interaction between student and teacher. Looking at the social and political ideologies of Black teachers in 1973, Lightfoot identified a 'hidden curriculum' which sought to empower and educate Black students.

Black teachers could relate to you better; they'd try not to show it but you would know. They would encourage you to try harder and they would talk to you on a personal level. They'd keep you back and talk to you. Mr Ashbourne was the only White teacher who behaved like that as well. (Michael, Marathon Boy, Wolverhampton)

He gave encouragement but it wasn't patronising. When he came with that type of vibe it was on a one on one kinda thing. It was not a speech that he prepared. It was very real, as if to say, I'll be cool with you, you be cool with me. He treated us like adults; I respected that. (Fabian, Relay Boy, Wolverhampton)

He was always giving us pep talks, advising us to work hard cos White people are not going to help you out, you got to do things yourself; any chances they get they will take you', and all that stuff. He was an outspoken teacher and like whenever we got into trouble he would say 'you're giving them a reason to kick you out of school, don't give them a reason, they gonna try to do that anyway'. He believed that they were always out to get you. It was funny though because as soon as a White person came into the room he would shut his mouth and as soon as they left he'd say, 'did you see how he was looking at me'. That's the type of teacher he was; he was funny. He just like tells you how it is. (Lester, Marathon Boy, Central Florida)

Where students share a common cultural background and engage productively with teachers, they are likely to be educationally motivated. The sharing of cultural solidarity was not, however, manifested in ways always welcomed by the students. For example, they found that Black teachers tended to be less tolerant of Black students' misbehaviour than they were of the White students; they '*came down harder on the Black kids*'. Trevor remarked:

He was mean [laughs]. He wouldn't tolerate anything from me. He had more of a relationship with the Black kids than the White kids, cos I guess he wanted to make sure they were doing the right things. He was tough but he was nice, he was a 'I won't tolerant any of your crap' kind of a guy. (Trevor, Marathon Boy, Central Florida)

Trevor valued his teacher's attitude, as he did not doubt that he had his best interests at heart.

Black male teachers as role models

These teachers were positive role models. One student expressed his pleasure: '*I was quite chuffed about that because I never saw any Black teachers before, let alone a Black male teacher*'. Others said: '*it was great just seeing him at the school*'; '*he was like a good role model because he was a teacher and he was Black*'; and '*he was a tremendous inspiration*'. The mere presence of Black male teachers gave inspiration to some of the boys but others needed to see more than their colour and gender.

It was very good when we had a Black male teacher, a Black male teacher that was strong, a Black male teacher that was intelligent, because we didn't not have many Black male role models in my neighbourhood or even in the school system. (Carver Relay Boy, Harvard)

Carver had high expectations of Black male teachers – they had to be 'good' teachers as well as good role models not just to compensate for the under-representation of Black male teachers in the school context but also the perceived lack of Black male role models in the wider society. Students were proud and felt encouraged by seeing Black male teachers being part of the school community.

All the students liked him, he was very good. It was positive to see one of your own in that position, he was good, and it made you want to achieve. Some pupils saw him as a cool teacher, you know the stereotypical image of Black teachers you see in the Hollywood films that raps in class, that's what people expected, but he was nothing like that. His attitude was 'don't talk to me about RMB, don't talk to me about your clothes, don't talk to me about anything like that, talk to me about your marks and I'll help you'. Only once did he let his guard down and talk to me about RMB, when he took an interest in the CD I was talking about. He didn't treat Black students any different. (Jestin, Marathon Boy, Wolverhampton)

He used to speak to the Black guys about how we need to do something positive with our lives; he wanted the Black guys to do really well. If the Black guys did something wrong in class, he would really come down on you, he would tell you how it is. He was a real inspiration. (Michael, Marathon Boy, Wolverhampton)

Black male teachers helped to affirm a positive sense of identity and enhance the boys' self esteem. Their presence helped students to shape their ideas about who can hold positions of authority and influence. Pupils who never see a Black teacher are likely to characterise the teaching profession and the pursuit of academic goals as better suited to White people (Blair *et al*, 1998). As Callender (1997) demonstrated, teachers who share similar cultural backgrounds, increase motivation, promote personal and academic achievement and instill a strong positive attitude towards learning. This was true for many of the students in this study, but not all had good experiences with Black male teachers. Opinions about them were mixed; some felt their expectations were not always met.

> Black teachers were good. They brought something different, e.g. African dancing and singing in assembly. In secondary school we had a Black male teacher; he was good at getting pupils' attention. He played different roles, sometimes he was on their side, other times he was on our sides; he was two faced. (Jakim, Marathon Boy, Wolverhampton)

> I didn't really consider him to be Black because he came from a different area; he came from the Midlands [laughs]. He didn't seem streetwise. I never felt he was on my level and in fact I felt he went out of his way not to look as though he was giving Black kids any preferential treatment, so he would never talk about race issues. He was a good teacher, but he was no different to the other teachers. (Bill, Marathon Boy, Oxford)

One should therefore not assume that Black teachers and particularly men are all the same. Each has his own views about teaching and how he relates to Black children. Black teachers in the USA were perceived to relate to Black children in a culturally relevant way rather more than many in the UK, who were inclined to treat all children the same.

Community Projects

Black community educational initiatives constitute a response by the Black community to their experience of racism in schools (Mac an Ghaill, 1988). Whilst some Black parents who are dissatisfied with mainstream educational provision chose to send their children back to the Caribbean to be educated, others, like some of the parents of students in my study, chose to capitalise on the opportunities available through community driven initiatives. The Black community in both the UK and USA have taken positive action to address the educational needs of their children by setting up programmes which supplement the educational provision of mainstream schools. More recently the USA has witnessed the emergence of the Black Male academy movement, which caters specifically for Black males. Although there is no equivalent in the UK, there are a number of localised programmes for Black males, and one national programme.

Collectively these programmes act as a bridge to enable Black boys to participate more fully in the wider society. Many of the students involved in my study had participated in mixed gender community driven interventionist programmes, including engineering programmes, summer academies, literary programmes and supplementary schools. In addition, some also participated in Black male programmes, including the 500 Role Model of America programme, the Union of Brotherhood, 100 Black Men and Black Boys Can.

One of the distinctive perceived benefits of these programmes was the exposure they gave the students to positive Black role models.

> I met a lot of people through that programme, people that I now see as positive role models. (Bobzy, Relay boy, Central Florida)

> It was good, we had to go out and meet Black professional men. (Lenford, Marathon boy, Central Florida)

> I could relate to the teachers better, maybe because they were Black. Some of them were qualified teachers, whilst others were members of the community. I believe the Saturday school also impacted on me because of the positive people who I was surrounded by as well. (Simon, Sprinter boy, Wolverhampton)

However, the main theme which emerged as a contributory factor to the educational achievement of these students was the pedagogy they were exposed to on these programmes. Students perceived these programmes to be '*an eye opener*'. Julius, for example, who attended Black Boys Can recalls:

> My mum and my Sunday school teacher encouraged me and my brother to go to Black Boys Can. It was a nice environment. It influenced my thinking about my ability to achieve and opened up new possibilities for me. We covered many areas ranging from Black culture to goal setting, and we learnt to cook as well. What I found most amazing was the lessons' we had on the Black presence in the Bible. That was the first time I ever learnt about Black people in the Bible so I found it fascinating. I also enjoyed lessons on Black inventors. Some I had learnt about though TV and Black history month, but a lot of it was new to me. I think we should cover these types of subjects in school. Our parents don't teach us these things because they didn't know either; they learnt British History at school, not Black history. (Julius, Marathon boy, Wolverhampton)

Julius' reference to the environment of Black Boys Can is a typical feature often noted in other studies about community interventionist programmes.

These programmes provided the boys with a strong group solidarity based on common experiences of being Black in a White majority society. The environments of these programmes are populated by positive role models coupled for instance with walls covered with images of Black success and inspirational posters, serving to inspire, challenge and empower the boys.

What is key in the pedagogy used in Black male programmes are that they promote: self-esteem, confidence building, academic values and skills, parents' development, community strengthening, transition into manhood and safe havens (Hopkins, 1997). These key features are part of a proactive pedagogy to counteract negative media stereotypes of Black men, stereotypes which affect how teachers and other authority figures make their decisions. These programmes provided a much needed supplement to the characteristically mono-cultural state schools curriculum.

Further insight into the pedagogy of mixed gender programmes in the UK, known as Supplementary schools in the UK are attended by both boys and girls. These voluntary schools have been in existence since the 1960s and are recognised for the way they provide invaluable educational and personal support for Black children.

> We learnt about things in the Saturday school that we didn't do in school, like Black history, cultural poetry reading etc and we also were taught certain lessons early, before they were taught in school, so I was ahead in some subjects, such as maths. At first I didn't want to go, but then when I went back to school and went through the same lessons', I realised how helpful it had been. It was a good experience; you just get more input basically. I know some people thought Saturday is your time, it's the weekend, but I actually liked going because I found it helpful. Everything they taught was more in-depth. (Simon, Sprinter boy, Wolverhampton)

Conclusion

Bourdieu's cultural capital theory provides a useful framework for explaining educational inequality but pays little attention to race related factors. Black boys are disadvantaged not only because they enter the education market without the relevant capital or because they do not manifest the same cultural behaviours as their teachers – which privileged children have learned but because of their race. The system is structured in favour of one class over another but also one race over another.

There were teachers within the system who instigated the factors that cause Black boys to achieve highly. A number were singled out for their effectiveness: they motivated their pupils and kept them focused, adopted unconven-

88

tional teaching styles, made lessons fun, interactive and challenging. Some teachers sponsored these Black boys emotionally through their professional concern and racial empathy. They understood and accepted the Black boys' identities. They believed in them, instilled hope in them and built up their confidence that they could achieve highly. They encouraged the boys, treated them equally, gave them opportunities to excel and expected a great deal of them. They displayed a strong commitment to learning, challenged them, provided them with personalised work and looked beyond the behaviour of even the most challenging students. By focusing on their pupils' talent and on maximising their potential, they were able to channel the boys' energies positively, so boosting their confidence. They gave the boys respect and commanded respect in return.

Despite being embroiled in the dominant cultural capital and its high status cultural attributes, codes and signals, these teachers had developed understanding of and appreciation for the tastes and preferences of Black boys. They used all this to engage them in education, thus preventing what Bourdieu calls 'self elimination', by which children choose to disengage themselves from the education system.

Black teachers can undoubtedly play a unique role in the educational lives of Black boys thanks to their shared experience of being Black in a White dominated society. But they have diverse views and diverse ways of relating to Black students and, as we saw, it was the African Americans who more often acknowledged the cultural identities of Black students and the challenges they face. Racial connectedness – taken for granted amongst White teachers and White children – does strengthen interpersonal relationships between pupils and teacher. This study found that the very presence of Black male teachers helped to affirm the boys' sense of pride and a positive sense of identity.

The Black community's interventionist programmes also provided the students with access to Black role models as well as giving the students access to a wide, culturally enriching and enhanced educational curriculum.

Irrespective of their gender or race, teachers play a critical role in the education of Black boys. They have to be trained to be able to respond intelligently to the multiple demands in the complex and changing environment of schools. Every teacher should be willing to learn the interpersonal and social skills that will enable them to get the best out of even the most challenging pupils. Many lessons can be learned from both Black teachers and White who, despite the broader school culture, contributed to the boys' educational achievement. Although Black boys featured among the 'underprivileged children' who were considered to 'present challenges to the educational system', these teachers rose to the challenge of effectively engaging this 'underprivileged' group in education.

8

Religion and its effect

The benefits of religion are often seen in the context of the afterlife. However, researchers have found that religion also benefits individuals in their lives and that there is a strong correlation between religion and academic achievement (Glaeser and Sacerdote, 2001; Glaeser *et al*, 2002; Jeynes, 2003). Jeynes found that religiously committed urban children performed better on most academic measures than their less religious counterparts, even when controlling for socio-economic status, race and gender. Similarly, Regnerus (2000) asserts that participation in church activities heightened educational expectations and achievement. He found that the more intensely religious students scored higher in standardised tests in maths and reading, irrespective of factors such as social class. This chapter explores various facets of religious influence on the educational achievement of the Black boys in this study, in particular their belief in God, and the social and educational influence of the church.

Stephen: a case study

Stephen is a Relay Boy from the University of Central England who took part in the pilot study. His account provides a useful framework for discussing key themes that emerged from my data.

> We were pushed to get an education in our church and educational achievements were always acknowledged. Church has helped me to stay out of trouble. Being a committed Christian, I don't get caught up in gang culture and things that my friends are drawn into, i.e. going out to parties and having late nights. This allowed me to have more time to devote to my education and to focus on the more important things in life.

I went to Sunday school from an early age. Sunday school was like an extension to school, but with a focus on the things which are more beneficial to life and your future, i.e. how to behave. I attribute a lot of my success to Sunday school. We had to read the Bible a lot, and in the Bible there is a lot of thou's and thee's, just as there is in Shakespeare. So when we did Shakespeare at school, we were already familiar with the language; this gave us a head start to many others in our class.

Our church puts on a lot of courses that are accredited such as the City and Guilds Teachers training course and e-mentoring courses run by various types of institutions like Bilston College and the University of the First Age. I got loads of opportunities for personal development that I wouldn't have been aware of had it not been for the church. My church also has strong association with an organisation called 100 Black Men, so two Sundays in every month kids from my church take part in their activities. They do things like leadership training and they get to see people who have made it in business and education...

We have at our church people from every walk of life – a mixture of lower-class and middle-class people and families. I am inspired by seeing so many Black professionals in my church. There's a guy here who runs his own company; I think, if he can do it I can do it too. My church provides lots of opportunities for interacting with professionals; there are lots of business people, senior executives, computer software engineers, accountants.... I think there is only one guy who is unemployed...

Being a Christian has developed my character. The only thing you have in the world is your character; people judge you by it, so if you have a good character you are guaranteed to get further in life ... I was taught that from a young age. If you go to our church and talk to the young people you will find that a lot of them have a lot of manners. They are kids at heart, but they also have manners. Because we are taught and live by Biblical principles – like the Ten Commandments, which instruct us not to lie, steal etc – we develop character and discipline. Also, because we have to sit still in church for quite a long time this develops discipline in us. When we had events like conventions – these are huge collective church events which start in the morning and finish at 10pm – we had to be disciplined [laughs], we just couldn't run up and down in church without getting into serious trouble from our parents. A lot of kids are not used to being in that kind of environment where they have to behave themselves for that length of time, but from the age of 2 or 3 years old, I had to. This helped to develop my character and caused me to be more disciplined.

Believing in God

Stephen, along with three quarters of the students in this study said that their religious orientation is a contributory factor in their educational success. Two of the students were Muslims, but all the rest who considered their religious beliefs to have contributed to their educational success were Christians. Christianity is the dominant religion in both the UK and the USA, and also amongst the Black population, but it is the American students who had the strongest religious involvement. Taylor *et al*'s study into racial differences in religious involvement (1996), for example, revealed that African Americans exhibit higher levels of religious participation than do Whites, and are considered to be amongst the most religious people in the world (Gallup and Castelli, 1989).

Of the few students who felt that their religious beliefs had no relation to their educational achievements, some thought that religion influenced them morally, but not educationally.

Like Stephen, more than a quarter of the students also used words such as *'focus' 'direction'* and *'guide'* when describing the role of religion in their educational achievement. Religion provided them with direction and kept them focused.

> I believe that if you keep on trying, you will succeed eventually, and even if you do not succeed, there will be something that you're meant to do. My faith really gave me a lot of inspiration when things got difficult. (Wilton, Sprinter Boy, Harvard)

Wilton's faith put him in a 'win win situation'; his academic pursuit would lead to academic success or to something else that he was destined to do. His faith gave him a quiet sense of confidence that his endeavours would not be in vain. Others were motivated by their belief that God expects them to do their best.

> Christianity has made me aware of my responsibility to make use of the talents I've been given by God. I love the parable about the master's coins, where the master distributed differing amounts of coins to his servants. He expected them to invest whatever he had given them and to yield an increase. However, the one who got one coin chose not to invest it, unlike the one who had been given several coins. When the master returned, he was angry with the one who had not traded on what he had given him, so he ended up taking it away from him and giving it to the servant who had traded well with his talents. I believe that God has given me talents which I need to trade on, i.e. I have been given certain potentials which I need to realise. I believe it is a greater crime of those who do not achieve because they waste their potential through slothfulness, laziness or lack of interest, than it is for those who do not achieve because they don't have the potential to achieve. It's a waste to bury what God has given you, no matter how small it is; that's just not good enough! (Henroy, Sprinter Boy, Oxford)

Religion provided these students with spiritual returns but also with secular returns and their belief shaped their educational value system.

Belief in the power of prayer

About a third of the students who cited their religious orientation as a significant factor in their educational achievement made specific reference to prayer and the role it played in their lives.

> I may look like a thug but I go to church at least three times a week. God is number one in my life; He is the Creator, He's why I'm here today. Every time I need something, I don't ask anyone, I go to Him and pray. (Albert, Sprinter Boy, Central Florida)

> I didn't worry about things as much. If there was anything troubling me, I'd pray about it. It gave me a sense of being in control. I sing in this acapella group that tours around the world; a lot of us are Christians, so we pray together. If anyone is having problems or feeling down, we'll take time out after rehearsals and pray and talk about it. I always prayed about my education and exams. (Erick, Marathon Boy, Oxford)

> I definitely feel God has helped me to be academically successful. I feel He is behind me, developing my mental skills, just making sure that I am protected and safe. I pray with my mother every night. (Dillon, Sprinter Boy, Harvard)

For many practicing Christians, prayer is a genuine form of communication with God. The reciting of prepared prayers is rarely part of public or private worship amongst Black Christians; rather the content of their prayers is personally constructed at the point of utterance. Prayer is perceived as a way to draw strength and solicit support from their direct relationship with God. Within the Black community, prayer is a valued form of capital (Pattilio-McCoy, 1998) but the importance of this non-dominant form of capital is, sadly, overlooked in the work of theorists such as Bourdieu. Prayer is part of the everyday life of Black Christians, particularly Black Americans (Ploch and Hastings, 1994; Gallup, 1996). For many students, God was like a fortress they turned to when there were problems. They believed that deity affected everyday life – not just life after death – and prayed for his intervention in their lives (Glaeser and Sacerdote, 2001). Religion gave them solace, confidence, strength and a sense of acceptance and belonging.

> Being a Christian has helped me academically. Just knowing that in times of adversity I have someone to look to, somebody to help me with the heavy burdens that I can't handle myself. (Arville, Relay Boy, Central Florida)

> When I was having trouble studying, I would pray and ask God to help me to be successful. It has helped me tremendously. (Brian, Marathon Boy, Central Florida)

> Religion has helped me through some rough times. I feel that God is watching when I'm having a rough time in class; this helps me; it makes it easier. (Kofi, Sprinter Boy, Harvard)

These students see God as immensely powerful and also as approachable, so they could go to Him for help. Like the participants in Channer's study, (1995), they see God as loving and caring, who provides hope and comfort when in distress.

The development of character and values

Like Stephen, their Christian faith helped to shape the boys' moral values. They feel that their religious beliefs have developed their character and shielded them from adversity.

> Without God, I wouldn't be here. Christianity has given me depth of character. I've looked at situations that my friends are in and know that I too could have been in them had it not been for God. (Sam, Marathon Boy, Wolverhampton)

> I feel I am able to resist peer pressure and I'm not as quick to jump into things because of my Christian values. I remain steadfast in what I believe. (Clive, Sprinter Boy, Harvard)

> Being a Muslim is more of a lifestyle, it stops me from getting involved in alcohol and drugs, and it helps me to be patient. (Tawanda, Marathon Boy, Wolverhampton)

Religion prevented the boys from becoming involved in crime, gangs, drugs and other immoral behaviour. It imbued them with strength and helped them resist peer pressure. Rather than adopting a pathological response to adverse situations, they were able to employ an adaptive strategy. Religion was a force that kept them out of trouble and on track to achievement. Ellison (1992) looked at specific aspects of the behaviour of Black Christians and found that African Americans who engage in prayer and Bible study, and for whom religion is important for moral guidance, are friendlier than other people. Although this study is not replicated, the findings raise an interesting point: were these Black Christian students exceptionally friendly and cooperative with their teachers and peers at school and, if so, did this contribute to their academic success?

A popular explanation in the literature for boys' underachievement is that they have low self esteem (Osborne, 1997a), although more recently (Spencer, 1991) scholars have demonstrated that it is Black males' self esteem within the classroom that is low rather than their general self esteem. Most of the students in this study were highly resilient, socially skilled, intellectually competent, self reliant and self accepting. Their strong sense of racial identity and their religious beliefs ensured that their self esteem remained high.

The influence of religious communities

Stephen considers the influence of his church to have helped advance his education. He belonged to a church with a strong pro-education culture which nurtured and developed skills valued within the school marketplace.

His church encouraged education, acknowledged achievement, acted as a satellite educational centre for mainstream educational institutions and linked up with community based educational programmes. Several other students also spoke about the pro-education culture within their church.

> My church used to reward us for doing well at school. They used to give out report cards to the kids, and if you got As and Bs they would give you a certificate and stuff like that. That helped to motivate us to do well. (Bobzy, Relay Boy, Central Florida)

> Our church highlighted our achievements. One of the things they did each year was they put up on the wall all the names of the graduates for that year, i.e. graduates from elementary school through to graduate school. They also published all their names in the anniversary book, and for the high school graduates, they would put their pictures up with a little profile and details about the college (university) they were going to. Sometimes they would call the students out to the front of the church and introduce them one by one to let people know what they were doing. We felt supported by the entire congregation. (Colin, Marathon Boy, Central Florida)

> If the church found out that you were not doing well, they would get on your case. My church was the biggest African American church in my neighbourhood. It had an education ministry with a board of teachers. Each teacher had a specialism, e.g. maths – who were responsible for looking over the students. Every Wednesday for about an hour and a half, we would have academic tutoring before Bible studies. We could sit wherever we felt comfortable, spread out and do our homework. It was like a hierarchy of learning; the Board of teachers would help the high school students and whilst they were doing their work they would help the middle school kids that were struggling. So we got help and we had to help as well. All the kids attended, i.e. about 50 to 60. Each week we would have tutoring first, followed by youth Bible studies and then choir rehearsal... so if you weren't there you'd miss everything. It was fun. (Trevor, Marathon Boy, Central Florida)

These quotes demonstrate the range of academic support provided by churches to students in their congregations. Although the boys attended a variety of churches, some ethnically mixed, a few predominately White and the majority predominately Black, it was the latter, particularly in the USA, that had a strong pro-education culture. The Black church is the oldest social institution in African American history (Cheatham and Stewart, 1993) and has been described as the anchoring institution in the Black community

(DuBois 1899; Lincoln and Mamiya, 1990) and as acting simultaneously as a bank, a benevolent society, a political organisation, a church hall and a spiritual base which culturally and religiously binds together the Black middle-class and lower-class (Pattillo-McCoy, 1998). In both countries, Black churches are among the few institutions owned and operated by the Black community, and education runs together with the formation of ideological beliefs and with social involvement (Putnam, 2000). The churches, particularly in the USA, have traditionally played an active role in addressing the educational needs of Black children.

Several of the students spoke as Stephen did, about having access to positive role models within their congregation. More often than not, the people who inspired them were professional Black men and women. The boys aspired to be like them and valued being part of a church community where they were able to interact with them. Students in both countries often cited historical religious role models, especially Martin Luther King. King was a Minister, a highly educated man and a good businessman. As leader of a civil rights movement based on peaceful resistance, he was a powerful force in overcoming segregation in the Southern States and affected race relations on an international scale (Shuker, 1988).

A place for skills development and nurturing

Stephen saw a connection between regular Bible reading and key educational skills. He maintained that regular exposure to the Bible made him familiar with the language which is used in great literature. He felt this gave him an advantage over peers for whom the language of, for example, Shakespeare, was hard to interpret. Other students also said the Bible was instrumental in their educational success: for some, it was the storybook read to them by their parents when they were children and even the book from which they were taught to read. The Bible had been a significant resource for developing various learning skills.

> I think indirectly my religion has contributed to my success. The Bible studies thing was huge; it was good practice for critical reasoning and vocabulary building. It also instilled work values in me. (Clive, Relay Boy, Harvard)

Bible reading extended the boys' intellectual capacity, introducing them to a wide range of conceptual frameworks, extending their vocabulary and developing their critical reasoning skills. Channer (1995) similarly found that church exposed her respondents to the philosophical and psychosocial aspects of life, taught them self discipline, and through encouragement, developed their work ethic.

Stephen spoke about the social skills he developed through regular church attendance. He believes that church attendance enabled him to develop a discipline which suited the classroom, for example, being able to sit still and listen for long periods. Glaeser and Sacerdote (2001) assert that sitting still and listening is a skill demanded by church and so the children become trained to sit and listen. Black majority churches also tend to have longer services than White majority churches.

These students perceived the religious community to have influenced their lives in profound and encompassing ways. It provided them with a strong personal, social and community identity, offered social and psychological benefits, and gave them a sense of belonging, reassurance and self validation (Channer, 19975; Rhamie and Hallam, 2002). Black churches are renowned for the care they give to their members (Calley, 1965).

Glaeser and Sacerdote (2001) found that although people's religious beliefs often decline with education, church attendance amongst the educated does not necessarily do so. They explain this apparent paradox with their finding that even if educated people's religious beliefs diminish, they continue to attend church for its social benefits. Whilst many of the parents of the students in this study did not have much cultural capital, the social capital which they had acquired through their religious communities contributed to their sons' academic success. Even single parents – with all the pressures they face in carrying out all that is expected of a 'good' parent on their own – effectively steered their sons towards academic success through capitalising on the social capital they had developed via their family network and often, particularly in the USA, the church community.

Concluding remarks

An overwhelming majority of these Black boys thought that their religious beliefs and the religious communities had significantly affected their academic performance, although the USA students had far stronger religious affiliation than those in the UK. Furthermore, the Black churches in the USA generally had a stronger pro-education culture and engaged in educationally focused social action. What has become clear, however, is that religion provided these students with a wealth of capital which they used to their academic advantage.

The Black churches gave the boys access to positive Black role models and provided them with a strong personal, social and community identity. The churches offered social and psychological benefits, and gave them reassurance, a sense of belonging and self validation. The church also provided indirect opportunities to develop educationally relevant social disciplines.

Religious affiliations also provided a rich source of cultural capital. Religious knowledge, competences and preferences could be deemed to be, in Bourdieu's terms, positional goods within the competitive symbolic economy. Some of the churches, particularly in the USA, had strong pro-education culture. The support they provided ranged from encouragement and acknowledgment of educational achievement to providing direct academic support. So students gained not just cultural capital through mixing with professionals including educators, but also access to cultural capital through the educational support and instruction given at the church. The Bible too was a source of cultural capital. Access to the Bible helped develop reading skills and exposed them to a certain language, extending their vocabulary and intellectual capacity. It introduced them to new conceptual frameworks, developed their critical reasoning skills and instilled a work ethic that disciplined them to work hard.

As well as cultural and social capital, belief in God and especially in the power of prayer, provided the students with another form of capital which cannot easily be categorised into any of Bourdieu's theories. If we extend the notion of capital to include non-economic forms, Bourdieu's theory of culture provides a rich conceptual resource; it paves the way for the conceptualisation of other forms of non-economic capital, including religious capital. Iannacconne (1984) used the concept of religious capital to explain patterns of religious beliefs and behaviour over an individual's life cycle, between generations and among family and friends. He understands it as a linguistic union of social capital and the notion of religion – a subset of social capital. Furthermore Putnam (1993) found that religion is by far the largest generator of social capital in the USA, contributing to more than half of the social capital in the country.

Yet the benefits these students gained from their connectedness to God does not readily fit into Bourdieu's social or cultural capital, nor Iannacconne's religious capital. Whilst religion may be a major factor in the formation of social networks, if one removes the social aspect there would still be some form of capital left which is unconnected to any of its dominant forms. The students stressed that it was their relationship with God that was central to their lives, not just the social affiliations formed through the church. They spent much time in private prayer.

Clearly, Iannacconne's concept of religious capital is inadequate to explain the connectedness to God which the students described and identified as contributory factors to their success. I have therefore coined the term 'Divine capital' to describe it. It is not a subset of other forms of dominant capital and is therefore a new form. A significant distinguishing feature of Divine capital is its lack of association with economic capital, whereas Bourdieu considers all types of capital to be fundamentally rooted – albeit concealed – in economic capital. However, Divine capital is fundamentally different because it is derived from a spiritual connection to God, and has no connections to economic capital. Divine capital has the capacity of enhancing both cultural and social capital. Access to God through prayer gave the students strength to apply themselves and gain whatever they needed to meet their social and educational objectives. Furthermore, they perceived prayer, a subset of Divine capital, as a valued form of capital. Prayer enabled them to draw strength and solicit support from God.

Although – according to Bourdieu – academic success is largely the preserve of pupils who are able to fit in with the dominant cultural values perpetuated through the school system, the students with Divine capital traded on their connectedness to God to embrace the dominant cultural capital, without rejecting other forms of non dominant cultural capital such as their Black identity (Byfield, 2007). Furthermore, Divine capital contributed to and enhanced cultural capital through encouraging the development of character and values suited to the educational market. Whilst neither social nor cultural capital relate to or enhance Divine capital, the possession of Divine capital could enhance both.

In summary, religion, though its provision of social, cultural, religious and Divine capital, enhanced these students' self confidence and imbued a sense of direction. This enabled them to remain focused in the face of peer pressure and difficulties, helped to develop their character, endowed them with moral values and shielded them from adverse situations and associations. Religion provided a psychological and social framework within which Black boys could make sense of their purpose in life, whilst providing them with emotional and social support to maximise their potential.

9

Personal qualities and navigational smarts

Earlier chapters considered the range of external drivers that helped the Black boys in the study succeed in education. This chapter explores the personal qualities that drove them on.

Intellectual capability

It is easy to assume that students who succeed are exceptionally bright. Yet only a few of the boys in this study considered themselves to be '*naturally bright*'. As Clive said,

> I'm not naturally bright, I'm not exceptional at all. I don't think I'm any brighter than my peers. I think I have had an amazing array of opportunities. (Clive, Relay Boy, Harvard)

Like Clive, most of the boys did not attribute their academic achievements to their intellectual ability. It is undoubtedly an asset, but the fact is that many gifted and talented Black boys still underachieve (Ford, 1995). Fabian, a Relay Boy from Wolverhampton University, observed that '*Most of my friends had the potential but ... um, none of them made it*'. Even a grammar school student from the UK who took part in my study initially failed to achieve the national standard of 5 GCSEs grade A*-C. He attributes his failure to the racism he encountered at his school – although he now acknowledges that he shouldn't have allowed that to affect his studies. Ability alone is unlikely to be enough for Black boys to succeed.

Hard work, personal drive and determination

About a third of the students attributed their success largely to hard work and their personal drive and determination.

> I have to work at it. I put the work in and then I get the results out of it. (Delaney, Marathon Boy, Harvard)

> I worked hard to get where I am today; it was a lot of nights in the library studying, but my efforts have paid off so far (Semore, Relay Boy, Harvard)

> I have to work hard at my studies, it's not something that comes naturally to me; I have to work at it. It's not just a matter of me sitting down and looking at a book and knowing that book inside out. When it comes to exams, I have to sit down and really plan my time and be organised. I've never been that type of student that works all the time. I would describe myself as someone who knows how to play hard and work hard. I would do as much as possible to get the best possible grade. I couldn't think of anything worse than coming home and telling my mum that I've failed something; that would be an embarrassment, especially when I know how hard she has worked to put food on the table and to provide for us. My mum and dad are not the most educated persons in the world, but they have drilled it into me that if you've got your papers [certificates] no one can tell you that you're only this or that. You can turn around and say 'I can do this or that and I've got the papers to prove it. (David, Marathon Boy, Oxford)

Boys like David strongly believed that hard work was essential for academic success and were motivated and determined. Even those from middle-class backgrounds, whilst acknowledging their privileged position, asserted that without their personal drive, determination and hard work they would not have made the grade. Goals and abilities were important but had to be accompanied by hard work. My study, like Ross's (1998), found that goal orientated students were far more likely to succeed because they focused on goal orientated behaviour. Most of the boys were driven, focused and worked hard. But some only learned the importance of the work ethic rather late in their schooling.

> I didn't really take my education seriously until the last five months before my GCSE. For my mocks I got Es and Fs. I used to do my work the night before or even in the morning. I'd quickly go and jot something down and hand it in. After my mocks I decided to knuckle down and to get organised. I'd talk to my sister. I used to just read, but she'd say, 'no, take notes, and highlight certain things'. She used to help me a lot. I started to do my homework early. I found that when I did that I had more time for myself. It was nice handing in good quality work; it was a good feeling getting good marks. It was a feeling I wanted. I started getting good grades every time. My confidence started to go up. I started moving up and my teachers started

giving me harder papers. I just knuckled down. I was shocked when I got my GCSEs; I ended up with mainly Cs. Although it was good, I know I could have done better if I hadn't left it until the last few months. (Michael, Marathon Boy, Wolverhampton)

Michael couldn't have obtained higher grades at GCSE because the English school streaming system had placed him in the foundation level. By the time Michael decided to start taking his GCSEs seriously, it was too late to move into a higher stream. The current GCSE framework with its emphasis on coursework and early streaming works against late developers and against last minute swotters like Michael. And Michael wasn't the only one who only knuckled down when they were about to take their exams. '*I realised that I had spent all this time at school I had to pass these exams otherwise I would have wasted all my time at school*' was a typical comment.

For some students, it was too late to gain academic credentials at the end of the compulsory school age. But they persisted with their studies, re-sat their exams and triumphed. Motivated by the belief that academic achievement produces social and economic advancement, they set goals, took action to meet them and then disciplined themselves and worked hard. One of the key points to come out of all of these accounts is that all the students had put in a lot of hard work.

Personal disposition
Self management
Some of the students attributed their success to their ability to manage themselves well.

I started to do most of my homework at school so that when I got home I could spend my time watching TV instead. I did my homework on the bus, on the way home etc just not at home, cos that was TV time. (Julieus, Marathon Boy, Wolverhampton)

I was surrounded by a lot of negative peer pressure but I was more for education, trying to go to a higher level. I did what it takes because I wanted to take advantage of the educational opportunities I had. I play football and I like girls, but I'm very disciplined, so I didn't let anything get in the way of my goals. I didn't focus on things that are not really important. I got my priorities right and I didn't let the outside stuff interfere in what I was trying to achieve. I motivated myself, I believed in myself, I knew I could achieve anything I put my mind to. I know a lot of people don't really like me because I'm Black, but I didn't really care, I tried to ignore it, think about me, what I'm trying to do for the next year, day, whatever; it's a mind thing, I didn't let it get to me. (Albert, Sprinter Boy, Central Florida)

I always made sure I was in the top two tiers at school. Even if I was at the bottom of the second tier I had to be in the top two tiers because then I could still push through. My mother used to tell me to 'shoot for the moon because even if you miss it, you'll still end up among the stars'. When I look at my educational career, that's just how I did most things, that is, I've aimed to be the number one in the class so that even if I dropped to number five, at least I'd still be somewhere up the top. (David, Marathon Boy, Oxford)

These boys used various techniques of self discipline. They motivated themselves, focusing on their long term goals and doing their homework. They avoided being distracted by racism, resisted negative peer pressure and positioned themselves in the top tiers in their class. They talked about making a conscious decision to restrict their social activities, as they believed too much socialising might adversely affect their focus and their academic career.

A competitive nature

A few of the students were driven to academic success by their competitive nature; they thrived on challenges.

I've always enjoyed being successful at more than one thing, being an outstanding student in maths whilst at the same time being outstanding in science. I wanted to, and still do, achieve the best I can; that's the goal of my education. Sometimes my stubbornness definitely comes in handy because when I have a problem, I keep on going, working at it until I resolve it. I just love challenges – facing them and defeating them. I love to bog myself down with extra curricular activities as it's when my time is crammed the most that I achieve a lot, so I always try to find as many things to do as I can and then aim to succeed in all of them. (Wilton, Sprinter Boy, Harvard)

I had a competitive nature. I wanted to be the best at things I set out to do. There was an invisible weight that would not be lifted until I conquered my next accomplishment. But then that was a cause of anxiety as I was a perfectionist; I would be very upset if I missed getting top grades in everything. I was a shy child so I had to keep being a smart child as my identity. (Neil, Sprinter Boy, Harvard)

A lot of people limit themselves, i.e. they want to be successful in their streets, as a Black person, as a South Londoner, but I wanted to be successful by national standards, by global standards. (Bill, Marathon Boy, Oxford)

I was keen on efficiency so I was keen on learning a process that would work for me time and time again. I wanted to know the best way to make notes, knowing the best way to revise, knowing the best way to do X,Y and Z. I believed that I could get myself into the top 10 per cent if I worked hard. At the same time I was determined not to overwork and give myself a nervous breakdown like some students do, so I was keen on learning to be efficient and to make the best use of my time. I've now got to the point where I almost enjoy doing exams, it's something to test myself against. I like to think that I have a formula that I can use time and time again. (Henroy, Sprinter Boy, Oxford)

Some boys' ambition related to education – they knew its value and strove for nothing less than top grades. For others, like Bill, striving for success extended beyond the academic realm into the wider society. In all cases, the boys who were driven by their love of challenge ended up at the top universities – Oxford or Harvard. Clearly there is a lesson to be learnt here: develop the habit of challenging yourself – it will pay off!

Self belief

These boys did not accept the claims of researchers such as Jensen (1969), Eysenck (1971) and Herrnstein and Murray (1994) that Black people are intellectually inferior and rejected such negative opinions of them. On the contrary, they developed a strong belief in their ability to succeed.

> I just believe that I am capable of doing whatever I put my mind and heart to. But then again, no one is going to believe in you unless you are already built up. If people do not see a new type of greatness in you then you will not receive any attention, so you have to believe that you are outstanding. (Carver, Relay Boy, Harvard)

> A lot of the stereotypes Black boys hear when they are young is that you'll never be this or that. Most people conform to it so easily because of the area that they grew up in. Drawing from history, I guess it's that plantation mentally that is still in most Black Americans today. I was born in Jamaica, so I didn't really know about Blackness and Whiteness until I came to America, so that was one thing that kept me out of that mentality. A lot of people rely on the crutch that 'I'm Black, so I can't do this or that', but over time I'm sure that mentality will go away. (Bobzy, Relay Boy, Central Florida)

Other studies also found that self belief characterised successful Black students (Wilson-Sadberry *et al*, 1991; Vispoel and Austin, 1995; Rhamie and Hallam, 2002; Rhamie, 2007). The confidence and optimism exhibited by some of these boys was consistent with their belief that the world is their oyster.

Capitalising on sport

A number of the boys were good at sport. It is fascinating to see how they used their sporting abilities to their advantage to obtain academic success.

> The 'goodies' didn't socialise or play sports. It was not cool to be in the hard working group, they were known as 'geeks', but as I got towards the end of school I got more into the hard working group. It was OK though, because I also played sports. (Synesius, Sprinter Boy, Oxford)

It was OK for me to get good grades because I played a lot of sports. The other kids who weren't sporty were seen differently, they were seen as 'geeks'. I was perceived as a jack-the-lad amongst the other kids but in an intelligent way, so it was safe to get good grades. I played rugby and that developed my confidence because I got to play against independent schools like Eton, and we beat these guys. It made us realise that they weren't so special after all. We interrelated with them on a friendly basis so it made me less frightened of institutions like Oxford, because we were exposed to the type of students who would go there. (Bill, Marathon Boy, Oxford)

Excelling in sport gave the boys street cred and this shielded them from being labelled a geek. Bill's sporting talent enabled him to mix with students from elitist schools, and winning games against them added to his self confidence.

Motivating factors

The role played by parents and teachers in motivating Black boys has been discussed earlier. But less predictable motivating factors were also at work and these are worth noting.

Learning from negative experiences

Several boys had negative experiences and encounters in their lives which could have discouraged them but instead made them even more determined to succeed.

My mum has lived a rough life and I just didn't want to go down the same path that she has been down [she lived a life of crime and spent most of his schooling years in prison]. Sometimes her lifestyle affected me but most times it just pushed me forward. It was a big motivator. I never want to end up in that situation. (Trevor, Marathon Boy, Central Florida)

I've been through a lot, I've seen a lot of guys who were in school drop out, seen a lot of guys who were good in sport but they quit because they thought they couldn't make it or succeed in life. I looked at things like that and it motivated me. I know a lot of people – even a couple of my aunties – who are on drugs really bad and that motivated me as well. I've been in situations where I didn't have anything, or my family didn't have anything and now we have something and we appreciate it even more. I motivate myself; I believe in myself, I know I can achieve anything I put my mind to. (Albert, Sprinter Boy, Central Florida)

I started to take my education seriously when I was 16. Before [then] I was going to school because my mum said I had to, but when I got to 16, I started working part-time at a grocery store and I saw these older Black men who had been working there for about 20 years, they were stuck there and were barely surviving. It caused me to look at myself and my own future. Then these men came at me saying the same thing – 'don't stop going to school, you need an education'. These men have been working all their lives and they don't seem happy and I have an opportunity to get an education to make more of my life. I knew then that I needed to start taking my education seriously. (Bobzy, Relay Boy, Central Florida)

I had an uncle who was bad. He left home when he was 15. He has nine kids. Everyone thought I was going to be like him just because I had his temper. He was my number one role model. During the time I dropped out of my 'A' levels, I was always at his place. But then I saw the reality of how he lived and decided I didn't want to live that kind of life, so when I went to college I started buckling down. (Michael, Marathon Boy, Wolverhampton)

I suffered from the middle child syndrome so I felt the need to prove that I was better than my sister; why, because of 'pride' and because I wanted to try to get back at mum and dad. (Fabian, Relay Boy, Wolverhampton)

Adverse circumstances had clearly made a lasting impression on these boys. They had heeded the mistakes of others – the imprisonment of one boy's mother, the drug addiction of aunties – and had learned from them. Other boys sought to learn how to avoid the dangers of not believing in themselves, or the poverty they had experienced as a child, and still others had been motivated by sibling rivalry. Interestingly, it was mainly the Marathon boys in both countries who testified to being driven by such hardships. They saw education as the key to avoiding situations of that kind.

Barriers in the labour market

Most of the students in my study believed that Black men face barriers in the labour market. But instead of this discouraging them, it drove them forward.

I know Black men face discrimination, that's why I am aiming to get more qualification so they can't say I haven't got this or that. (Simon, Sprinter Boy, Wolverhampton)

We are at a disadvantage, but we can help ourselves. We know we're going to struggle regardless so why not try to do our best while we are struggling. You can work for the Whites without an education and make $10 an hour or you can work for the Whites with an education and make $100 an hour; that's the way I look at it. (Lester, Marathon Boy, Central Florida)

There's no secret that Black men face barriers in the labour market. Nine times out of ten your bosses are going to be White and people you're in business with are going to be White. It's going to be harder for me as a Black guy when I apply for a job. You've got to try harder, that's just the way it is, so don't get upset about it, you've just got to face up to it. (Jestin, Marathon Boy, Wolverhampton)

These boys' perception of discrimination in the labour market just made them more determined . According to Farrell (2004), a key difference between those who achieve academically and those who don't is that achievers recognise a link between working hard at school to get academic qualifications, and future success. As one student so succinctly put it: *'Ten room mansion, that's what drives me!'*

Personal strategies
Working secretly
Some of the boys who were strongly committed to achieving high academic credentials kept very quiet about their ambitions.

> I read a lot of newspapers and watched Newsnight, so I always liked discussing political issues in school. I got into trouble a lot because I was always challenging the authority but then I wasn't interested in being in the teacher's good books. I enjoyed learning because it meant people couldn't pull the wool over my eyes. My view of the education system was that it was geared towards maintaining the status quo. I saw myself as being left wing as a kid because I had read my brother's sociology textbooks. I saw school as a place where they would make sure certain kids succeeded at the expense of others. That's how I felt for a long time. My goal therefore was to make myself so intelligent I could break through the system. That was the plan. At that age I was quite impressionable about political ideas. I had read a lot of Marxism. I was pro-education as long as I can remember, but my academic performance at school could be quite variable in that it was conceivable that I could fail a lot of my GCSEs. It wouldn't have surprised people if I had failed. They didn't see me as someone who was focused, but they knew I could do well if I did what they wanted me to do. I saw my brother not play the game and lose, and my sister not play the game and lose. Oftentimes I didn't want to play the game either, but I did know what I had to do, so come exam time, I played the game. I went under cover and worked hard. (Bill, Marathon Boy, Oxford)

> Even though I was doing my schoolwork, I was still going outside and talking to everyone. Because I didn't just hang around with the smart people, people didn't think I was really smart so I didn't get called names like 'teacher's pet' or 'nerd' and I never showed anyone my report. When I graduated, I was amongst the top 10 per cent in my school. People would never have guessed that I would have achieved that. (Bobzy, Relay Boy, Central Florida)

> Throughout my school years it was good to get good grades, but you couldn't show that you tried to get good grades, otherwise you'd be seen as a goody goody – that's how it was. I would hang about with everybody in my neighbourhood, and also the Black guys in my school who were in lower grades, but I was independent. They'd be surprised at the grades I was coming up with. Every time I got my report

card, they'd say 'oh my god, you're so smart'. People were shocked because the attitude I gave off and the way I appeared to be so relaxed, they thought I was doing the same thing they were doing, but I wasn't, I took my education seriously. (Lester, Marathon Boy, Central Florida)

Bill resembled students in Mac an Ghaill's study (1988) who were determined to get a good education even though they didn't like school. However, unlike the Caribbean student in Gillborn's study (1990) who avoided teachers he was likely to get into conflict with while remaining publicly committed to his studies, Bill made no such effort. Bill received detention after detention for his insolence to teachers (see Chapter 5). He had become politically aware at an early age and his political views, shaped by Marxism, made him want to beat the system which, he believed, was geared toward maintaining the *status quo*. As a Marathon Boy from a lower-class background, he was determined to get a good education because he believed he had the right to it – although he did not always study as hard as he should have. Bill did not want others to know that he was working hard so he studied secretly.

Bobzy, too, hid his hard work. His multi-layered smokescreen – socialising widely, not hanging around only with the smart kids, and keeping his reports from his buddies eyes – shielded him from being teased by other children for being a geek. Meanwhile he got on quietly with his studies.

According to Fordham and Ogbu (1986), Black students who succeed academically are at risk of being accused of acting White and being cast out by their Black friends. Lester's friends, unlike Bobzy's and Bill's, were predominantly Black. But Lester exemplifies how some Black boys worked hard at their studies, pursued their goal of academic success and still managed to keep their Black friends. In one sense, Lester did not play the game of concealing the fact that he was working hard, but he did play a game of shielding himself from criticism whilst he got on with his work, by not hanging out with the geeks. Black boys like Lester were adept at creating a middle path where they maintain their friends whilst pursuing their ambitions.

Black boys played other games with their friends in order to achieve. Like Lester, they avoided '*sitting with the boffins*' and pretended that they didn't enjoy studying when they were with friends who were not keen on working. It was again mainly the Marathon boys from poorer family backgrounds in both countries who had to learn to play strategic games of concealing their commitment to their studies. Sprinter boys tended to go to good schools where it was acceptable for all students to work hard, so it was easier for them to be open about their efforts.

Navigating friendship groups

Rather than having to work surreptitiously to achieve their academic goals, some boys took care to choose friends who would not stand in their way.

> I was in the top set. The girls worked but the boys didn't do that much. By year 10 and 11 I spent more time with girls because all the boys wanted to do was play football, every waking minute. Every Black boy I knew played football and I didn't want to play football. (Julieus, Marathon Boy, Wolverhampton)

> In middle school, my friends didn't like school at all, but I did. But then I found some kids who liked school as much as I did. We eventually became goods friends. I maintained the old friends but made new ones as well. The old friends were Black males; the new friends were White females. (Trevor, Marathon Boy, Central Florida)

> In elementary school I wasn't fussed about my friends but by the time we got to 11th grade I just started to hang around with kids who saw things my way, like my friends that were going to college. They were going to do something with their lives. I stopped hanging around with people who had no ambition. (Bobzy, Relay Boy, Central Florida)

> When I decided to change [from his rebellious ways], I decided to sit in a different place in the classroom. From that point onwards I made different friends. My schooling became very different and my behaviour totally changed. I use to sit at the back of the class, but I changed seat. That was the turning point for me that helped me more than anything else. (David, Marathon Boy, Oxford)

> When the thug mentality became popular – expressed in their dress and language – the Black guys became almost like convicts. This is part of the reason why I didn't have many Black friends at school. (Docky, Sprinter Boy, Central Florida)

> It definitely wasn't good to be doing well, especially if you were a boy, it wasn't good at all, but I didn't care. I loved controversy so I didn't mind being picked on. Instead of making me want to be like them, it kinda drew me away from them. (Henroy, Sprinter Boy, Oxford)

> I always wanted to learn but it was difficult because I had a lot of friends who felt otherwise, but I didn't follow them. I sacrificed a lot to get my education. (Freddie, Marathon boy, Harvard)

> Up until our third year in secondary school some of my friends were good athletes and good students, but when we got into our third year, I noticed the rapid decline in the Black boys' performance. Attendance started to drop back and they didn't have any focus on what they wanted to do when they left school. Some started to become drug dealers and gang members. I too got caught up in the 'I can't be bothered attitude'; I lost focus. When I realised that I was getting caught up in that way of life I took the decision to walk away from them. (Jestin, Marathon Boy, Wolverhampton)

Henroy was one of a few of students who was unpopular for wanting to do well at school, but this did not deter him from following his academic dreams and he displayed excellent coping skills.

More often than not, however, the boys chose friends who were also ambitious and used friendship strategically. Some changed their friends completely and even befriended White girls. Some kept their existing friends whilst making friends with academically ambitious students too. Some changed their seats in the classroom to surround themselves with hard workers, and resisted adverse pressure by walking away from the peers they regarded as a negative influence.

Like the students in Farrell's study (1994), these boys chose to reject not only some of their friends' values but the erstwhile friends themselves. Although some of these boys did waver briefly in their commitment to their studies, all eventually decided not to allow anyone to undermine or thwart their academic efforts. Their self reliance enabled them to move in an independent, constructive direction based on their goals and principles. As Edwards and Polite (1992) observed, self reliance is an attribute which separates the leaders from the followers and the innovators from the conformists. It indicates the ability to set your own direction and 'move to your own beat rather than to the rhythm of others'. And these boys had an abundant of self reliance.

Concluding remarks

The students who achieved academically succeeded not just because of positive influences in their lives but also because of their own determination. Operating from a position of racial strength, these boys were not going to rely on their parents or teachers to gain them the success they wanted. A common thread runs through their stories: all of them, be they a Sprinter boy, Relay boy or Marathon boy, from the UK or USA, worked hard to achieve high grades.

Some of the boys were driven to academic success by their competitive nature, others by their belief in themselves and yet others by their desire to get out of poverty. They were determined not to let anything stand in their way, not even their friends. Some became skillful at managing their friends, playing strategic games to conceal their pursuit of academic goals. They developed an amazing ability to balance their academic efforts without jeopardising their friendship with less academically ambitious friends. Only a few were ostracised by their friends for studying hard and those who were coped well.

More often though, the boys selected their friends to ensure that they mixed with pupils who were also aiming high. Some had to make the difficult decision to change their friendship groups totally, whilst others widened their friendship groups. Some literally repositioned themselves in the classroom among the ambitious students and repeatedly resisted negative peer pressure. The students exhibited great self reliance, which helped them to pursue their goals. The Relay boys and especially the Marathon boys were the ones who had to learn to play these strategic games, because they were more likely to live in poor neighbourhoods and to mix with boys who scorned education and succumbed to pressure in the hood.

The Black boys in the study were outstanding; they took charge of their own lives. They organised their time well and disciplined themselves to study. Those who were good at sport exploited their prowess, capitalising on the status it gave them to liberate them to work hard instead of letting it distract them from learning.

PART FOUR
PROGRESSING INTO HIGHER EDUCATION

10

Going to university

I n both the UK and the USA, the number of Black students attending higher education has risen (Modood and Shiner, 1994; Nettles and Perna, 1997) yet Black men are still under-represented in higher education. Much research is focusing on university access or ethnic minority students (Modood and Shiner, 1994; Modood and Acland, 1998), but little is specifically concerned with Black male students. This chapter explores the issues surrounding Black boys' progression into higher education. It identifies the factors that influenced those in my study to attend university and their rationale for choosing particular universities. Although my study did not set out to examine Black male students' perceptions of elite universities or the views and experiences of those who attend them, the interviews produced useful data on a scarcely researched area.

Searching out a university
Significant others

It was parents and school teachers who most influenced these students' decision to pursue higher education.

> From the age of about 11 my mother was always saying 'you go to school, go to college and then go to uni', but it wasn't until my last year of GCSE that I really decided to go. (Michael, Marathon Boy, Wolverhampton)

> My parents went to Harvard so there was an expectation that I and my younger brother would also attend Harvard. There's a picture of me at home, aged 3, in a Harvard jacket. They wanted me to go to a top-notch school so my grades and extra curricula activities had to be right to ensure that I could. (Neil, Sprinter Boy, Harvard)

I hate to say this, because it sounds cheesy, as he was an immediate source of authority, but my history teacher made a big impact on me. He was the first from his family to go to uni and was keen on seeing those who could do well do well. He encouraged me to apply to Oxford. Also my English teacher informed me about an open day in Oxford and suggested I attend, so I went. (Henroy, Sprinter Boy, Oxford)

Marathon Boys were significantly more likely to cite their parents as their greatest influence whereas Sprinter Boys cited their school tutors as well as parents. Sprinter Boys generally attended private schools or 'good' schools in middle-class neighbourhoods where progression into higher education was expected by the school and thus echoed the parents' expectation.

This study found that the parents of Sprinter Boys were more likely to encourage them at an early age to consider university. Some therefore never made a conscious decision; it was a natural progression, almost an extension of school. As one boy said: *'I was just born into it, it was never a decision!'* Such students' career paths tended to be mapped out early on and they were familiar with the education roadmap they would follow in order to turn their childhood dreams into reality. However, although some of the Marathon Boys' parents had also always wanted their sons to attend university, the boys were less likely to aspire to university until much later. It wasn't until they were nearing the end of compulsory schooling that they embraced their parents' vision, as in Michael's case. This finding highlights the importance of a shared vision between parents and schools and the importance of that vision being reinforced at school.

The choice process and the instruments employed

Students entered the choice process with the belief that *'university will open up opportunities for me to get higher level jobs'* and *'it's a place for gaining useful contacts for jobs and to meet influential people'*, but they did so at different stages in their schooling. It has been argued that a student's university choice process starts younger if they are academically able (Hossler and Gallagher, 1987) or if they are White (Litten, 1982). But most of these able students did not decide to go to university until quite late, except for Sprinter Boys from both the USA and the UK.

The Marathon Boys generally undertook significantly less research into universities than the Relay or Sprinter Boys, except for those who chose Oxford, who tended to examine league tables not just by university but also by course ratings. Paulsen (1990) identified parental educational background as one of the most significant factors in students' choice of universities by university and also course ratings. The parents of Marathon Boys and, to a greater extent, Relay Boys were far less likely than the Sprinter Boys' parents, with their greater cultural capital, to be involved in the research process. Abraham and Jacobs (1990) and Horvat (1996) found, as I did, that a few students were influenced by older siblings who had been to university and also by alumnis.

Some students visited the universities.

> You know what it's like when you just go to a place and it feels at home, it feels warm; I felt I could take my shoes off, that's what it felt like when I stepped unto Central Florida's campus. (Arville, Relay Boy, Central Florida)

Site visits were conducted especially by Sprinter Boys, who possessed both cultural capital – so knew the value of such visits – and economic capital -so could afford to travel long distances to view universities. Other students relied upon information from careers advisors, successful professionals, prospectuses, the progression routes of alumnis and league tables. League tables were the single most popular mechanism for gaining information about the quality of universities, but were used by less than a quarter of the students. Marathon Boys and students from new universities were significantly less likely to examine league tables.

Most of the Marathon Boys and others from lower-class backgrounds in both countries either considered elite universities to be beyond their reach or had negative perceptions of them. It took some critical incident to make them apply.

> I would have been 14 or 15 when I really heard about uni. In the case of Oxford, there was a leaflet going around the class, I started reading it but my teacher looked at me as if to say 'you'll never get in there'. He had a son who went to Oxford. That was the thing that challenged me to apply to Oxford. I wanted to prove to him that I could get in if I wanted to. That particular teacher had tried to embarrass me publicly in class before and all the class started laughing at me. I was angry that he had done that but it made me more determined and more focused. (Bill, Marathon Boy, Oxford)

> Initially, I did not want to apply to Harvard. A lot of people back home saw Harvard as elitist and White. My two top choices were Columbia (an Ivy League university) and Moore House (a Black university), but then one day the Harvard recruitment board sent me an e-mail introducing me to Harvard. They followed it up; they called me. I was sceptical, but I applied and got called for an interview. It turned out that the interview went extremely well, but I was still sceptical. Then they invited me to FROSH [an event for all the students who had been offered a place]. Just being

here was an experience; it was the total opposite of what I expected; I realised Harvard was an opportunity of a lifetime. (Delaney, Marathon Boy, Harvard)

Like Bill and Delaney, Marathon, Relay and Sprinter Boys from lower-class backgrounds said it was a critical event that led them to apply to an elite university. One student remembers seeing a poster at his sixth form college inviting students who were interested in applying to Oxford University to attend a special class. Another was invited to an Open Day by a teacher, and yet another was struck by a talk from an Outreach Worker from Harvard University. None of the Marathon or Relay Boys, with the exception of two, would have applied to an elite university had there not been these fortuitous interventions. Typical comments were: '*I never thought about applying to Oxford in my life*', '*I would never have applied otherwise*', and '*the Outreach Worker made me realise that Harvard is accessible*'. Unlike the students from good schools, these boys received little or no help with their application or their personal statements and had no mock interviews. As Hugh reported:

> All my research into universities was done independently. I looked at about 15 or 20 universities. I checked out different courses and the entry requirement. I didn't have any form of preparation; my preparation was in effect to work hard at school and not let anything sacrifice my grades. (Hugh, Sprinter Boy, Oxford)

Criteria for selection
Geographical location

The geographical location of universities was a factor for a third of the students. Whilst some of the students from Central Florida had opted for a university in a warm state, most of those who cited location as important were referring to the proximity to their home: '*I wanted somewhere local because I didn't want to have the responsibility of getting a house*' and '*I need to be near my family*'. Modood and Shiner (1994) and Taylor (1992) found that a disproportionate number of minority students make applications to their home regions and the findings from this research support this. Localism was more significant for Marathon Boys and those from lower-class backgrounds. Localism is a race as well as a class issue – in the UK, 40 per cent of minority students are located in London universities, primarily the 'new' universities (Preece, 1999).

Given the choice of these four universities, it appears that the boys were not keen to attend universities that were '*too much in the woods with nothing going on*' or '*out in the sticks, somewhere with no life*'. Access to a vibrant city life influenced Erick, for instance, to opt for Oxford rather than Cambridge.

Cambridge is a lovely town but it's very university centred. I went there once outside of term time and there was just nothing going on. I'm from South London and that's busy and hectic, so Cambridge just wasn't the type of place I wanted to live in; it was just too different. I wanted to go somewhere where, if I wanted to escape from university, I could; I could go out to a bar and not see anybody from college or university. There's just more life in Oxford and so much more diversity as well. (Erick, Marathon Boy, Oxford)

Cost

Cost was one of the dominant factors in the higher education selection process for the students in this study, as in the studies by Freeman (1999) and Sevier (1992).

My parents played a strong part and also my high school counsellor in selecting a university, but in the end it came down to who was giving me the most money. (Docky, Sprinter Boy, Central Florida)

Didn't really think about going to uni until I had finished college, and then I didn't really want to go, to be honest, but the choice was to sit around and do nothing or get a job. It was the sheer cost of going to uni and the debt I would end up with that I found off-putting. I have taken out a student loan, I work part time and my parents help me with my fees. In my second year I got a grant. My parents say I should stop thinking about the money, but I didn't really want to be a burden on them, even though I knew they would pay for it. (Simon, Sprinter Boy, Wolverhampton)

Financial considerations powerfully affected many of the students' decisions but differed in the two countries. UK students were expected to fund their studies largely though government initiated student loan packages. Some, like Simon, were reluctant to accrue a debt. But they managed to overcome this reluctance by focusing on the long term benefits of gaining higher academic credentials. As the government controlled and standardised university fees for undergraduate degrees throughout the country, choice for the UK students was never based upon course fees, although it was at times influenced by the cost of living away from home. By contrast, USA student's choice process was directly influenced by the fees, which vary considerably, the more prestigious universities charging the most. Marathon Boys and those from lower-class backgrounds were often looking to obtain a degree by '*the cheapest route*', so the availability of financial aid was an important consideration.

Since African American families are over-represented amongst low income earners, Black students are more dependent on financial assistance (Clark and Crawford, 1992). Scholarships are given primarily by state, so students saw it as in their financial interest to attend a university in their home state. This largely accounts for the high proportion of students from Central Florida who chose to attend a university in their home state. Harvard University, however, is one of the exceptions; it offers scholarships to students irrespective of the state they are from. Those from lower-class backgrounds got 100 per cent or nearly 100 per cent scholarships.

Ethnic mix

Just over half the students expressed a preference to go to an ethnically diverse university because '*it's always nice to have people who you can relate to; it's just nice to see a Black face*'. However, this preference was not always aligned to their final choice, which was often determined by other considerations.

> Harvard has such a reputation for being the best college ever, so I associated Harvard with the best education I could receive, a place where I could be cultivated to the optimum. However, one of my concerns was that I would loose touch with my Black community, maybe I would sell out – but then my education, my experience, knowledge and understanding of Black culture prevents me from doing that. So once I realised that would not be a danger, then I knew I could go ahead, I could go to Harvard. I think that this would be a place where I could accomplish my desires, which is helping ameliorate inequality in society. I like the attention too. At first when I got offered a place at Harvard I had doubts and fears: maybe I was not intelligent enough, maybe I was a sell-out. But then I placed my fears into perspective as I realised that each step that I take would be a step on behalf of my ancestors who were not allowed this opportunity, I'd be taking a step on behalf of all the people who believed in me, taking a step on behalf of all my community, taking a step for all those around the world who cry out for salvation, liberation and hope. All those things compel me today; they keep me believing, they keep me striving for success. (Carver, Relay Boy, Harvard)

Carver was obviously influenced by the reputation of the university. Unlike the students in the studies of Allen (1987) and D'Augelli and Hershberger (1993), who were concerned about being able to adjust to a culturally diverse environment, Carver was afraid of loosing his Black identity. Only by maintaining a view of the long-term benefits could Carver opt for Harvard. Their university choice was framed for many of these students by their desire to retain their racial identity.

The course

The availability of their chosen course was a major criterion for selection amongst the students, whatever their country, social class or cultural educational heritage. Some – particularly the Sprinter Boys – looked beyond the course content to its structure and the department. Hugh, in common with many others, acted in the belief that a university that has an excellent reputation for a specific course will enhance their career prospects.

> I chose the course first and then the university. I looked at the course structure, the modules, the teaching staff and the reputation – not just of the university but also the department – and then I tried to picture myself there; would I be happy? (Hugh, Sprinter Boy, Oxford)

Status

Unlike Sevier's (1992) findings that Black students rated the reputation of the university as strongly affecting their choice, I found that it was mainly the Oxford and Harvard students who took the university's status into account.

> I came to Harvard because of the name recognition. Name recognition plays a huge role. A lot of times you can just say 'Harvard' and before they ask you what you majored in, they accept you. (Wilton, Sprinter Boy, Harvard)

> I looked at Oxford first and then I looked to see if it offered a biology degree. Whatever was in the degree I'd do it, because it was Oxford. I think it is the wrong way to go around picking a university, but then – maybe it sounds a bit pessimistic – because I am Black, I am likely to struggle in the job market, but I know that if I have an Oxford degree it will make life easier for me. (Tony, Sprinter Boy, Oxford)

Whilst gaining access to a high status university is an end in itself for some students, others perceived status to be synonymous with quality teaching. Hugh, for example, said:

> I was concerned about the quality of the teaching rather than the status. In the long run status is also determined by the quality of the teaching and in turn a lot of good teachers are attracted by the status. (Hugh, Sprinter Boy, Oxford)

It was rare to find a student from Harvard or Oxford who had applied to a new university. They believed that people should try to get into the best university they can '*because it's worth more*'. The brand name of elite universities was expected to act as a ticket for career advancement and social mobility: '*just the name 'Harvard' will increase my options and open up a few doors*'. In addition, they also expected elite universities to open up opportunities to meet students from families with influential contacts. Furthermore, for students from lower-class backgrounds, like Carver, gaining access to an elite university was perceived to be not just a personal achievement but an achievement for the Black community. Some of the students even sacrificed the course they wanted to do in favour of a less competitive course in order to increase their chance of getting into Oxford. This strategy was particularly noticeable amongst those who wanted to pursue a career in law. Their game plan was to obtain a place at the University and do a law conversion course after graduation.

Elite universities: perceptions and experiences
Perceptions

Some of the students from the universities of Wolverhampton and Central Florida had not considered applying to an elite university, while others had consciously decided not to.

> They're not for me. Why, it's the kind of people that are there, not because they are White but because of their class, you know, posh people with rich mums and dads. I just couldn't see myself around those kinds of people. (Simon, Sprinter Boy, Wolverhampton)

> I'm not really a 'work, work, work' type of person; I have other interests apart from studying which I would also want to give some attention to. The people who go there are workaholics and if I went there I would have to change and I don't want to change; it's kind of fun being me. Oxford and Cambridge are very elite universities. They do let a few Black people in but you have to be the cream of the crop, and although I am the cream of the crop I'm not their type of cream of the crop. My social and political beliefs would be different to theirs. (Julieus, Marathon Boy, Wolverhampton)

> I know my grades wouldn't have been good enough plus I wanted to go somewhere where I can get a diverse experience. For me, the people who go to those schools (universities) are totally opposite to me, they want to be the next President, but I don't really want that, I just want to live comfortably. The amount of focus they have to put on education would make me go crazy; I want to be able to relax at some point in my college career. (Bobzy, Relay Boy, Central Florida)

Some students doubted that they would get the grades elite universities required or did not want to devote all their energy on academic work. Others, notably students from Central Florida, would have liked to have gone to an elite university but were prevented by the cost. Few knew about the financial packages available from universities such as Harvard, whose policy is to accept students on academic grounds rather than the ability to pay. Indeed, all the students in this study from lower-class backgrounds who attended Harvard were in receipt of 100 per cent or nearly 100 per cent scholarships from the University.

However other students – mainly the Marathon Boys and those from lower-class backgrounds – chose to exclude themselves from elite universities because they did not see themselves 'fitting in', or, as one put it, '*I don't think I would feel at home there, it's not my world*'. There was clear evidence of psychological constraints on their choice – they regarded such universities as the domain of the middle classes. Reay (2001) showed how social class impacts on university choice, asserting that choice is in part a process of psychological self exclusion in which elitist universities are often discounted. Bourdieu notes how objective limits become transformed into practical anticipation of such limits, leading one to exclude oneself from places from which one is excluded. By excluding themselves from elite universities, students were exhibiting a Bourdieurian sense of place, of 'one's relationship to the world and one's proper place within it' (Bourdieu, 1984).

Students' experiences

Although some of the students from Harvard and Oxford had been surrounded by stereotypical views about elite universities, they still chose to apply. Erick, a Marathon Boy from Oxford University, for example, was led to believe that '*they're really posh*' and '*they all wear tweed*' at Oxford, but says he wasn't put off by the stereotypes but went and saw the university for himself. Bill's case description offers useful insight into the experiences of Black male students at elite universities.

Bill

When I got dropped off in the taxi to come for my interview I heard posh voices, voices that I had never heard before, except on TV.

For many of the students, I was the first Black person they had experience of interacting with, so initially some of them were a bit shy towards me. I found this a little uncomfortable. I always wondered whether they held any stereotypes about Black people. However, I soon found myself teaching them about my culture and they were teaching me about theirs. There was only one other Black person in my college.

I never received any racial abuse; I've always felt safe and happy. I've never been a fan of the idea that being a good teacher means being colour-blind; it's about recognising the differences that people have and I felt my tutors at Oxford did that. They didn't make ridiculous effort to make out that I was just another White middle-class kid; it was more like 'we understand you are from this background, what can you bring to us'; I felt this gave me confidence. A big difference between Oxford and school is that Oxford had a high expectation of me right from the start. Everyone who comes here is used to that, but for me, that was a big, big difference. When I was elected president of the Student Union for my college, my philosophy tutor sent me a postcard congratulating me but also advising me to aim for the top grades.

What helped me to succeed here is my ability to network. When I arrived here, it was easy to become selfconscious and go into a shell because I seemed to be the only Black person here. I had to adapt to that new environment whilst also being able to revert to my old self when I went home and to communicate with my old friends at the street level. You have to be able to do this otherwise it can become difficult because if you can't relate to people on the street level then you would just be regarded as another Black kid who went away and lost their roots; I wanted to avoid that psychological hang-up.

I am constantly being intellectually challenged at Oxford. I have met people here that I thought I would never have met in my wildest dreams.

One of the things I've learnt at Oxford is social etiquette, which is very different to manners. You can be considered to be a gentleman even though you are not a nice person, because you know what cutlery to use etc. That's why I love it here, because it trains you to be able to play the game. There are a lot of formal occasions which can be off-putting; they make you feel like less of a person if you can't do what they do. When I graduated, you could see those guests who were uncomfortable in the social surroundings ... some of them did not know how they were expected to use their knives and forks. If my younger brother had come to my graduation ceremony he probably would have found it very off-putting, although Oxford is not really like that on a day to day basis; in the dining hall everyone just tucks into their food.

There are times when I just try to blend in, I don't put on an accent but I do talk a little more posh like they do. The problem with me now is that I'm losing touch with the street slang and that happens as you get older. I'm beginning to loose the words, but listening to hip-hop helps me a little. I still stay in touch with my old friends.

Students like Bill are a minority in elite universities in terms of both social class and race. His account offers both a Black male perspective and a class perceptive. Bill echoes the perception held by many of the students from new universities about elite universities being middle-class institutions. In fact most of the students at Oxford did have middle-class backgrounds and 'posh voices'.

Galis (1993) asserts that the culture of elite universities is alien to students from lower-class backgrounds and that to succeed in them academically and socially demands habits of mind and conduct of which class is a greater determinant than race, gender, national origins or sexual orientation. He likens the experience of a student from a lower-class background entering an elite university to being like taking a kid out of a hollow in Appalachia and transporting him or her to another planet with no life support. Yet like Bill, most of these students adjusted socially to this utterly new environment. They now had to meet the social expectations of the disparate social worlds of the *'streets back home'* and the university and adapt to both worlds so they could *'blend in'* at the university and still *'relate to people on the street level back home'*. The ability to culture switch was essential.

Not all the students escaped criticism for losing touch with their culture. One reported that not all his friends were happy about him going to Oxford and that this made life difficult back home, because his friends thought he was *'arrogant'* or *'think I'm only being friendly because I don't want them to think I'm arrogant. Either way'* he concluded *'I can't win'*. Fries-Britt (1998) asserts that not only do most Black students in White majority universities experience isolation on campus but they are also likely to experience isolation from the Black community. However, their families, the church and the wider Black community were generally proud that they had got into an elite university.

> My mum is so proud of me. She always tells people that I go to Harvard, which angers me a lot. It irritates me because sometimes when people hear the name 'Harvard' they tend to place you in a cocky category and I don't like that. Some people feel intimidated by me now, but I know I am respected. I try and keep a low profile in my community back home; I don't go out on the streets a whole lot to just relax. My friends' attitude towards me going to Harvard is a bit like my mother's, they keep on telling people. It annoys me so I tell them to stop it. (Dillon, Sprinter Boy, Harvard)

Generally the students found their communities supportive. They had to contend with jovial remarks from friends, such as *'Oh I suppose you won't be talking to us anymore'*. But they didn't want to be treated differently, to be *'put on a pedestal or brushed aside'* – they would be uncomfortable if the people around them felt inferior. Some felt that their community perceived them as *'being emblematic of hope'* and *'embracing pupils' aspirations'*. One remarked *'I'm like a mini celebrity when I go home, they're so proud of me'*. Two of the Harvard Marathon Boys intend to return to their home towns after graduation to contribute to their communities but neither wishes to go back permanently because their *'horizons are wider now'*.

Students from new universities feared the workload the elite universities would impose and this perception was confirmed by students who did go to Oxford or Harvard. This is precisely why a student from Oxford University was critical of people who hold the view that Oxford and Cambridge universities shouldn't be seen as being different to other universities; he put it down to their sheer ignorance of the amount of work that is expected of them. He added '*I have friends who go to very good universities like Bristol and UCL and they're not doing a fraction of the amount of work we do here yet they are doing the same course as me. They appreciate that I do more work here at Oxford*'.

In earlier studies, students – particularly those from neighbourhoods and schools with high ethnic minority populations – were found to experience 'culture shock' when attending an institution where they are the minority (Allen, 1987; Person and Christensen, 1996). Some found themselves on the receiving end of racism for the first time. However, most of the students in this study had lived and been to schools in ethnically diverse populations or were emotionally prepared for being a minority in a university setting, so did not report culture shock. However, not all the students at Harvard and Oxford were as lucky as Bill; they spoke about encountering racism. One reported that stereotypical views were held of Black students at Harvard. Another was uncomfortable when tour groups visiting Harvard '*would look at me as if to say 'what are you doing here?*'' One student at Oxford occasionally felt he had been on the receiving end of racism, mostly from students rather than staff.

However, virtually all those who went to Harvard or Oxford enjoyed their university years. They welcomed the high expectations of the lecturers and the excellent teaching. Teaching staff at Oxford, in particular, were praised for '*going out of their way to help you*'. The students felt intellectually challenged and privileged to have met people they would otherwise never have encountered.

The Harvard students gave enormous credit to the Black Men's Forum – a student society for Black male students – for helping to make their experience of Harvard so positive. The Black community at Harvard was seen as welcoming and very strong and so '*one of the most cherished and comforting aspects of Harvard*'. One student who initially wanted to attend a Black university described the Black Men's Forum as '*a micro Moore House*' (a very successful Black university). The students found it '*uplifting to get together once a week with other Black men from Harvard*'; it was where they found camaraderie. They particularly enjoyed the discussion forums, social events and the networking opportunities it provided. As one student put it, '*you have many people networking and this is really awesome*'. Fries-Britt (1998) affirms the benefit for Black students to establish successful connections with others who excel academically as it provides meaningful peer relationships and supports their racial and academic identities.

Preparing for the real world

Some of the students in my study had already begun to think about their career prospects following university. Whilst there was some optimism, fed by the knowledge of the value of the academic credentials they were on target to obtain, they were somewhat sceptical too. Some foresaw obstacles in the labour market, due to racism, and were already making plans to overcome them.

> Me and my friends were talking about the employment barriers only yesterday. We were saying that when we go for a job, we are tempted not to declare our ethnicity. It's getting better, but it's still hard. (Brian, Marathon Boy, Central Florida)

> People have stereotypical views about Black males. I and my family changed our name so people can't tell by our names that we are Black. You've got to get an application through the door before you can get an interview. (Tony, Sprinter Boy, Oxford)

> Because of the reality of racism in the labour market, I wouldn't pursue a career where networks are very important. I would never consider being a barrister or even pursue a career in banking as these types of career prospects are heavily racialised – you'll never be a criminal lawyer. Being a politician and being Black is very difficult. I would love to challenge that, but to some extent I'm afraid that some people will simply vote against me because I'm Black. (Hugh, Sprinter Boy, Oxford)

It was mainly the UK students who expressed concern about their future prospects. Even those at Oxford doubted whether impressive academic qualifications would prevail over racism. Their views echo those of Edwards and Polite (1992), who argue that 'what this new Black generation so well primed for achievement would ultimately learn is that even when one is qualified, success is not always guaranteed, for there remains continuing obstacles – from within and without – to opportunity; success still means to gain academic credentials and then to be ready for the struggle'.

Concluding remarks

This chapter has shown that shared aspirations and encouragement by parents and schools to go to university were significant influences in deciding to pursue higher education. Students with such backing were more likely to have planned to attend higher education and to choose their university when quite young. Older siblings who had been to university and also alumni influenced the students' decisions. Where parents' aspirations for their sons to pursue higher education were not reinforced at school, the boys were at risk of not proceeding to higher education.

A variety of criteria were applied to selecting a university. As found by Abraham and Jacobs (1990), Sevier (1992) and Freeman (1999), the cost of the course was important and, for the USA students, so was the availability of financial aid (Clark and Crawford, 1992). The geographical location influenced the boys from lower-class backgrounds who preferred to stay local. Neither geographic location nor costs were major factors in the middle-class students' choice. Although Allen (1998) found that the ethnic mix of the higher education institution influenced Black students' choice, my study suggested that diversity was seen as desirable rather than essential. Students were more interested in sustaining aspects of their ethnic identity than whether they could adjust to a culturally unfamiliar environment (Allen, 1987; D'Augelli and Hershberger, 1993). The course content mattered but whereas Sevier (1992) found that Black students also took great account of the university's reputation, here this was true only for those who opted for Harvard or Oxford and wanted to increase their social, cultural and economic capital.

Choice reflects both power and stratification (Giddens, 1995); students make different kinds of choices according to their circumstances. Except for course fees, which are more or less standardised throughout the UK but vary hugely in the USA, there were few differences in the boys' choice processes. Students in both countries were constrained by their predicted and actual grades so only those with high grades could consider an elite university but even then, some students, primarily Marathon Boys, were too concerned about 'not fitting in' to apply. Social class opens doors to certain students and also restricts them to certain types of universities. Marathon Boys who ended up at an elite university did so only after something made them realise its accessibility.

The students' choice processes depended not just upon their academic ability (Hossler and Gallagher, 1987) or their ethnicity (Litten, 1982) but more on their family's educational background and social class. For Marathon Boys and to a lesser extent, Relay Boys, choice is limited by finance, their poor information about higher education, and their preference for ethnically diverse and local institutions.

Marathon Boys who accessed an elite university experienced culture shock, but this simply developed their skills in culture switching between the two worlds in which they now belonged. In addition to class tensions, these students also experienced tensions within their home communities. Although not immune from incidents of racism, almost all the boys enjoyed their university experience: the high expectations of the lecturers, the intellectually excellent and challenging teaching and the comradeship of organisations such as the Harvard's Black Men's Forum helped to facilitate these experiences.

With no family history of higher education participation, the Marathon Boys and, to a lesser extent, the Relay Boys, tended to work on the surface level of choice because of their unfamiliarity with certain aspects of choice known only to the Sprinter Boys.

PART FIVE
CONCLUSION

11

Implications for policy and practice

This book set out to determine:

- Whether Black boys in the USA and UK who achieved well at school and go on to higher education have been exposed to the factors known to correlate with the underachievement of Black boys

- What factors contributed to the educational success of the students in this study

- What influences successful Black boys' access to and choice of universities

This final chapter discusses the discrete yet interrelated obstacles the students faced during their schooling and the factors that helped them overcome those obstacles. Although Bourdieu's cultural capital theory has been a dominant paradigm in terms of its application in the lives of many of the students involved in this study, his ethnocentric bias takes no account of the numerous ways in which the cultural resources of Black groups are converted into capital. A few sociologists have distinguished between dominant and non-dominant cultural capital (Lamont and Lareau, 1988; Hall, 1992): 'dominant cultural capital' corresponds to Bourdieu's high status cultural attributes, codes and signals, and 'non dominant' to the tastes and understandings accorded to a lower status group, and their preferences in linguistic, musical or interactional styles. Both types of cultural capital are of value, depending upon the field in which the capital is used, although non-dominant cultural capital may not be symbolically legitimised. My study shows that non-dominant cultural capital explicitly and implicitly influences the lives of the students.

Social class

Social class has long been considered to affect academic achievement. Half the boys in this study were from lower-class backgrounds and typically had uneducated parents who held low paid jobs and lived in poor neighbourhoods, often characterised by dilapidated houses, failed businesses, high unemployment, crime, drugs and violence, prostitution, shooting and fighting, poorly resourced schools and low rates of attainment. However, social class is not a separate issue – it is a vital thread that goes right through this analysis. Cultural capital played a significant role in the organisation of class differences – even between the boys in this study – and helps to explain how social inequalities are organised in the culture-drenched societies of the UK and USA.

Personal factors
Black boys' subculture and the laddish culture

I agree with the aspects of Bourdieu's theory which purport that educational success entails a whole range of cultural behaviours, extending to ostensibly non-academic features like accent. Privileged children have learned the accepted behaviours, as have their teachers, and they fit into the world of educational expectations with apparent ease, unlike underprivileged children, who are considered to be difficult and to present challenges. Indeed the non-conformist attitude and behaviour associated with the laddish culture (Bleach, 2000) and Black male subculture (Majors, 2001; Sewell, 1997; Kreisberg, 1992) are deemed to be factors in Black boys' underachievement. Most of the students in my study were surrounded by laddish culture – that is, by peers who devalued education, who assigned feminine characteristics to those who were pro-school and who labelled and targeted pro-education students – and moreover many of them were themselves active members of that culture.

Coupled with this, there was much evidence to support Kreisberg's theory (1992) that schools are sites of ongoing conflict and struggle for control for Black boys. Some of the boys' resistance to domination was evident from their truancy, their conflict with both teachers and schoolmates and all the detentions and suspensions they incurred. Moreover, many Black boys come not only from lower classes and are thus what Bourdieu calls 'underprivileged', but come also from an underprivileged ethnic group. So it is not surprising that most of the students, whatever their background, displayed non conformist behaviour at school. It is not just the laddish culture but also Black male subculture that clashes with the culture of UK and USA schools. However, unlike the Black youths in Majors and Billson's study (1992) whose survival strategy was 'Cool Pose' – a non dominant form of cultural capital – most of the students in my study adopted alternative strategies which did not compromise their academic goals. These are discussed below.

The schooling system in both the UK and the USA has been held responsible for Black boys' dis-identification with academics, a factor found to lower their attainment levels (Osborne, 1997a; Fordham and Ogbu, 1986). Yet my study found that whilst there were certainly teachers which the boys did dis-identify, there were also teachers whom they singled out – White as well as Black – as having earned the 'right to be listened to'.

In the boys' eyes, these teachers had symbolic capital. They were highly motivated and enthusiastic about teaching, had unconventional teaching styles, made their lessons fun, interactive and challenging, kept their pupils focused and motivated, took a personal interest in them, were racially aware and accepted the boys' identities, instilled hope in them and built up their confidence in their ability. They encouraged them, treated them equally, gave them the chance to excel and had high expectations of them. They demonstrated a strong commitment to their learning and challenged them through the provision of personalised work. They looked beyond the students' behaviour to locate and focus on their talents, channelling their energies in a positive way which in turn bolstered their confidence. They gave them respect and in return were respected.

Black teachers were important to Black boys, giving them a sense of cultural connectedness which helped to develop good interpersonal relationships and to prevent them from dis-identifying with academics. The very presence of Black male teachers was inspirational, affirming a sense of pride and a positive sense of identity. This was particularly true of the teachers in the USA, who were more assertive about acknowledging the cultural identities of their pupils and their challenge of being a minority in White dominated society.

The tensions of meeting the demands of their peers

Theories that Black boys experience tensions between their endeavours to do well academically and at the same time keeping in with their peers have been identified as one cause of underachievement (Majors and Billson, 1992). My study found this phenomenon mostly pertained to the students who were low in cultural capital. Their parents' cultural capital largely determined the type of school they attended and this in turn influenced the educational values of their peers. Those who went to 'good' middle-class or private schools encountered less adverse peer pressure. The students affected by such tensions played strategic games with their peers, such as concealing their hard work, carefully selecting who they sat next to in class, navigating their friendship groups, choosing friends who would validate their academic orientation and censoring themselves when they were with friends who were not academically orientated, creating smokescreens to shield themselves from their ridicule. Some boys developed an amazing ability to balance their academic pursuits without jeopardising their anti-education friends. Others completely changed their network of friends, building a form of social capital with students who had similar academic values and thus avoiding the negative peer pressure described by Fordham and Ogbu (1986). Few were ostracised or sanctioned by their peers for being pro-education and the few who were demonstrated excellent coping skills.

The tension between maintaining their identity and 'acting White'

Drawing on oppositional cultural theory, Ogbu (1998) and Fordham and Ogbu (1986) postulate that being pro-education is regarded as 'acting White' – conforming to the dominant cultural capital – thus creating tensions between maintaining their Black identity and being accused of 'acting White', with adverse effects on academic attainment. It may well be that Black boys recognise the importance of dominant cultural values in society but have difficulty juggling dominant and non-dominant cultural capital. But relying only on non dominant cultural capital to maintain their cultural status reduces their social mobility. Whilst my study found evidence of this tension generating some non-conformist behaviour at school, only a few students, mainly from the UK, lacked a strong sense of Black identity. Most chose not only to maintain their racial identity but to strengthen it.

These students did not consider the word 'dominant' to be synonymous with 'superior' and could distinguish between dominant and non dominant cultural capital and embrace both. They successfully juggled both forms of cultural capital, negotiating strategically between their community, family, peers and schools. They embraced the achievement ideology associated with dominant cultural capital, although they resisted the cultural default of this ideology – such as White middle-class standards of speech, dress, musical tastes and interactional styles (Carter, 2003) – whilst simultaneously embracing Black cultural capital. This enabled them to acquire valued status positions within the wider society for their achievements and also within the Black community for not, at the same time, selling out. Rejecting their cultural identity for academic success was a price they were not prepared to pay. The maintenance of Black cultural capital enabled them to operate from a position of racial strength and thus overcome the barriers to their success.

Knowledge of the labour employment market

Black boys are well aware of the discrimination in the labour market and this is thought to discourage them from trying to achieve at school (Fordham and Ogbu, 1986) but the students in my study were undeterred. On the contrary, it spurred them on, making them determined to acquire the cultural capital they needed to overcome whatever barriers lay in their way. The students in the USA were more optimistic about their future prospects than those in the UK, due partly to the country's more visible Black trailblazers and professionals. These students took charge of their own lives. Their personal drive and determination, strong work ethic, self belief, ambition and determination to overcome obstacles all contributed to their success.

Self esteem

A popular theory in the literature to explain Black boys' underachievement is that Black boys have low self esteem (Osborne, 1997), although more recently scholars have demonstrated that Black males' self esteem may be low in the classroom but high elsewhere (Spencer, 1991). As this is not a psychological study, it was difficult to determine the boys' level of self esteem. Suffice to say, they were characteristically resilient, socially skilled, intellectually competent, self reliant and self accepting. And amongst the mélange of factors that positively influenced their lives was their strong sense of racial identity and their religious faith.

Although Bourdieu does not include religion in his definition of various forms of capital, my study showed that religion engineered a form of capital which positively supported the educational attainment of these boys. In many cases the church – particularly the black churches in the USA, which had a strong pro-education culture and engaged in educationally focused social action projects – provided these students with a strong personal, social and community identity. It offered social and psychological benefits and access to positive role models. It imbued a sense of belonging, reassurance and self worth and provided opportunities to develop educationally relevant social disciplines. The churches encouraged, supported and celebrated educational achievement. And reading the Bible regularly, a practice strongly advocated in these churches, helped develop reading skills, exposed boys to historical language, extended their vocabulary and their conceptual frameworks, and developed their critical reasoning skills.

In addition to the cultural and social capital drawn from the church, their connectedness to God provided these students with another form of capital: Divine capital. Divine capital enhanced their self confidence, gave them a sense of direction, helped them to remain focused in the face of peer pressure and disappointments, developed their character, enhanced their moral values and shielded them from adverse situations and crime. In the USA especially, faith has historically been the force that has enabled Black people to overcome structural, legal and institutional obstacles. In the lives of these students, Divine capital has been pivotal to gaining academic success.

Racism and related issues

All the main forms of racism highlighted in the literature, including pupil racism (Troyna and Hatcher, 1992; Gaine, 1995; Sibbitt, 1997; De Lima, 2001) teacher racism (Gillborn, 1990; Sewell, 1997; Blair *et al*, 1998; Watt *et al*, 1999) and institutional racism (DfES, 2004) was evident in the schools of many of the boys. Whatever their country, social class, educational cultural heritage or university attended, all but two reported being subjected to racism during their schooling. Some found support from their schools but others had to cope with it as best they could, sometimes in ways of which the school authorities disapproved. However, some teachers were positive towards the boys and my study also highlights the high expectations some schools had of their students – a factor also identified as important in other studies (Rhamie, 2007; Rhamie and Hallam, 2002; Day, 2004; Blair *et al*, 1998). I found that resources and facilities were good in most private schools and schools in middle-class White neighbourhoods. But such schools, in line with Bourdieu's theory, perpetuated class inequalities. It was mostly their students who gained admission to an elite university.

Parental involvement

I found that the involvement of many parents of these boys were not much different from that of parents of Black boys who underachieve. The parental involvement in the education of their sons that is often recognised by teachers – that is, professional labour at home and being visible at events such as Parents Evenings or Parent Teacher Associations – requires parents to have resources and knowledge about the subject matter being taught, which not all these parents had. Given that most of the boys' parents had little cultural capital that they could convert into such assets, they could be deemed to be 'failing'. But this was not how their sons saw them. All the students thought their parents had significantly contributed to their educational success. And contrary to Bourdieu's assumptions, all the parents, irrespective of their social class, saw education as a key to social mobility and prized it highly.

However, my study aligned with Bourdieu's theory that power and ideology are central to differential achievement, since the parents who had cultural capital could provide their sons with greater cultural advantages. They were able to translate their cultural capital into power, confidently challenging their sons' schools when they were dissatisfied. Much evidence was found to support Crozier's (2000) ideas that social class relations impact upon parent school relations. Parents from lower-class backgrounds were noticeably more distant and marginalised from the school than middle-class parents. However, Bourdieu's assertion that middle-class parents have a more comfortable relationship or fit with the school may not be true of Black middle-class parents, as I found them to be far more likely than working-class parents to have conflicts with the school.

My study challenges the oversimplification of parental involvement discourses which glorify certain forms of parental involvement at the expense of others. Irrespective of the cultural capital, all the parents actively participated in their sons' education, albeit to varying degrees. Being immersed in a pro-education value system and proactively engaging in and exploiting the school market for the benefit of their sons – especially in the UK where parents had more choice – cut across country of origin, university type, social class, family structure or indeed the social, cultural or economic capital of the parents.

The degree of cultural capital possessed by parents was played out in the type and level of their support. Those with little or no cultural capital provided less direct support to their sons, particularly as they progressed through school. And although most made strategic efforts to send their sons to the 'best' school, their cultural capital tended to frame their school choice. Few parents who had little cultural or economic capital sent their son to a private school; it was mostly the parents with strong cultural and economic capital who opted for the high achieving schools in their affluent neighbourhoods or for private schools.

Parents' reasons for not attending parent meetings differed according to their social class. Time constraints were even more severe for the parents from lower-class backgrounds in the USA, some of whom had more than one job, whereas middle-class parents often chose not to attend because they found the meetings unproductive – it was they, and not the school, who decided when to engage with the school.

Whilst single parents were less likely to send their sons to private schools, engage in conflicts with their son's school or to expend professional labour in the home – particularly as their sons got older – they nonetheless employed compensatory strategies in pursuit of their sons' educational success. For example, they instilled strong educational values in their children and effectively capitalised on the social capital they had developed via their family network and, particularly in the USA, the church community.

In summary, these parents employed a diverse range of strategies to support their sons' education, not all of which were the traditional ones. What they had in common was a strong commitment to education. These students perceived that it was their parents' values which underpinned so much of what they said and did in their pursuit of educational achievement.

Going to university

Their academic success at school meant that the students could progress into higher education. They chose which university to attend according to criteria which were closely aligned with their cultural capital. The cost of the course and the availability of financial aid were important for the USA students who had little cultural capital but not for those with strong cultural capital. The UK students were influenced by the cost of pursuing higher education generally and whether or not they could afford to live away from home. The geographical location was significant for students with low economic capital in both the UK and USA. They generally chose to stay close to home, primarily for financial reasons but also because they wanted easy access to their much valued social capital – their family.

The ethnic mix of universities was also a major consideration for some students from both countries, particularly amongst students from lower-class backgrounds who were keen to sustain their ethnic identity in an ethnically diverse population. Course content was also important and a few students also took account of the course structure and the reputation of the department offering the course. Students who were endowed with cultural capital and keen to increase it put much store in the reputation of Harvard or Oxford.

High grades afforded students wider choice, and many of the highest achievers opted for an elite university. But some with high grades, primarily those with little cultural capital, did not apply to such universities because they were anxious about fitting in to universities populated by middle-class White students. Cultural capital enables or limits an individual's entry into high status social groups, organisations or institutions (Bourdieu and Passeron, 1973) and this was the case with these students.

Students from families with strong cultural capital, who had attended 'good schools', were far more likely to be confident and achieve the grades required for Harvard or Oxford. And they were comfortable in these settings, as they were used to being educated alongside White middle-class students. Those with less cultural capital had to learn to adjust to a 'foreign' social class setting and to develop the social skills to culture switch between the two worlds in which they now belonged. It took a critical incident to break this pattern, such as a teacher being dismissive about a Black male student possibly getting into an elite university and firing the student to prove them wrong.

The Black boys in this study have successfully accessed higher education, but there is certainly no room for complacency and no guarantee that they will be able to achieve the social mobility they want. As Bourdieu reminds us, the value of all forms of capital, including cultural capital, are constantly being renegotiated in implicit and explicit ways, so as players in the market acquire more capital, so such capital becomes devalued.

Bourdieu's theory of cultural capital is only partly played out in this study. Grenfell *et al* (1998) point out that we should not get carried away by the apparent determinism of Bourdieu's theory as there is always choice. But in reality, their cultural capital strongly influenced the students' choice.

Yet many of them succeeded in getting into higher education and in some cases elite universities despite having poor cultural capital. I found that a supportive family anchored the boys in every case, especially when combined with a supportive school, strong religious affiliation and the desire to succeed. When surrounded with people – schools, parents, peers, church and community – who share the same values and high expectations Black boys are far more likely to do well.

If, as Bourdieu maintains, schools play a major role in social elimination – that is, progressively removing pupils who are deficient in cultural capital from access to higher knowledge and social rewards – then the Black boys in my study are impressive. They not only managed to survive the school system but succeeded in it against the odds. The boys from families with little cultural capital who obtained a place at one of the world's most highly respected and competitive universities – Harvard or Oxford – are truly exceptional. In addition to social class disadvantage and the laddish culture – which affects many boys, these boys also had to face what Edwards and Polite (1992) call 'the Black tax', in the shape of race related barriers.

The final challenge

This book has exploded the absurd notion that Black boys are a homogeneous group. Each is different and their schooling experiences are diverse. The school system presents enormous challenges; hard work alone is not enough to guarantee success. All the key stakeholders – the government, schools, teachers, the community, parents and the boys themselves – have a part in determining whether they succeed. The recommendations below for education policy makers and schools are neither prescriptive nor exhaustive so are not intended as a blueprint for addressing all the challenges faced by Black boys. Rather, they are recommendations based specifically on the findings of this study. In some cases the distinctiveness of the practices is a matter of emphasis rather than of kind.

Central education policy

■ League tables have always been controversial. They are seen as indicators of the highest achieving schools, as they give the raw scores of examination results. It is the rawness of the scores that so distorts the picture. The best schools are those in which the pupils, whatever their attainment at entry, make greatest progress so the basic premise of league tables is flawed. The second major problem with league tables is their incompatibility with stated government concerns on both sides of the Atlantic to deal with the persistent gaps in achievement between the successful and the unsuccessful students – which includes most Black boys. The recent US commitment to the principle of *No Child Left Behind*, and the UK's *Every Child Matters* are inimical to the present system of league tables, making a rethink essential.

■ The dearth of substantive knowledge about academically successful Black boys indicates the pernicious underlying assumption that these boys are anomalies. Policy makers need to re-evaluate the policy documents concerning Black children and avoid propagating a deficit view of Black boys as underachievers.

■ Being poor affects where one lives and the quality of educational provision. Such structural barriers can hold Black boys back. So there is an urgent need to establish strategies to reduce structural inequality for economically underprivileged groups in both the UK and the USA. Recent initiatives such as charter schools in the USA and academy schools in the UK are presented as part of educational reform aimed at addressing educational disadvantage. These new forms of schools may be hospitable to innovation and best practice. However, the effectiveness of these schools will be significantly enhanced if due account is taken of the wider structural impediments including the social and physical landscape of poor neighbourhoods. The new schools need to be reinforced by and integral to a wide local regeneration programme if they are to effect change.

■ Race equality laws and policies have existed in both countries for years, yet Black boys are still having to face educational challenges. Consequently, radical policies are needed to address racism in schools. Race equality and cultural diversity training should be made compulsory for school governors, school leaders, teachers and support staff and should be part of national teacher training programmes, so that all those working in education can respond constructively to multiple demands in a complex and culturally diverse environment and meet the educational needs of Black boys. Race equality should be an obligatory integral part of educators' continuous professional development.

Schools

■ School leaders will have to be bold enough to review their school culture and ethos critically and objectively, and to provide a strong lead in, and rigorously monitor, race equality. Racism in schools – be it institutional or personal – must be tackled, as it interferes with the pupils' learning. Racist incidences should be acknowledged, recorded, monitored and addressed and pupils should never be left to cope with racism on their own but should rather be able to feel confident that their schools will not tolerate it. To overcome the challenges of institutionalised racism, an independent Race Advisor should visit the school each week to provide a listening ear, and to advocate on behalf of students who are subject to racism.

■ Schools in both the UK and the USA need to review their curriculum in light of the culturally diverse society. Those which do have culturally related lessons should review their curriculum content and quality to ensure that they give a rounded picture of Black culture and history and do not just focus on topics such as slavery.

■ Teachers need to take responsibility for improving pupil-teacher relationships and incorporate interpersonal relationship strategies into their teaching to ensure a balance between the affective and technical aspects of their work. Teachers need to move beyond the rhetoric of listening to and valuing all students to actually doing so, teaching through their actions as well as didactically. If they are to gain Black boys' respect and enhance their motivation, confidence and performance, they must demonstrate a strong commitment to their learning, provide them with personalised work, set them challenging goals and support to meet those goals, locate and maximise their talent, channel their energies in a positive way, develop cultural competences and an understanding of their culture and identities, give them opportunities to excel in class and celebrate their successes.

- Events such as African American or African and Caribbean achievement evenings can provide opportunities for pupils to celebrate their achievements and feel proud of being African American or Black British.

- The value of Black teachers needs to be recognised. Schools need significantly more Black teachers – particularly men – who can connect culturally with Black boys. The governments should provide incentives for schools to recruit more Black male teachers. And Black teachers in the UK need to be empowered to express their cultural identity at school, as the Black teachers in the USA do.

- Schools need to change their mindset towards parents and regard them as partners and also customers: it is not only the pupils who need to be treated with respect but their parents also. Schools should conduct customer satisfaction surveys to solicit the views of the parents on a range of matters, including Parents Evenings, the schools equal opportunity polices and the curriculum. Contrary to the stereotypical views held of Black parents, my study highlights the strong educational values held by Black parents, irrespective of their cultural capital.

- Schools should form genuine partnerships with Black parents and give them the information and support that will enable them to enhance their role in their sons' education.

- Parents and pupils need to be given full information about higher education.

- The contributions of the Black community, particularly the churches, to the lives of Black boys indicate the need for more community driven interventionist initiatives that offer a wide, culturally enriching and enhanced educational curriculum to complement school based provision. Models of best practice and the pedagogy of community educational programmes should inform mainstream schools.

■ Schools should work in partnership with community educational providers and the Black-led churches to help children develop a strong Black identity and learn more about their racial and cultural heritage so they can operate from a position of racial and spiritual strength. Having such strength enabled the students in this study to navigate their way successfully through the school system.

■ It is imperative that schools have high expectations of Black boys and align their potential with their achievement. The effects of their high expectations should transcend the boundaries of school so that the students are given the choice to opt *out* of university – opting *in* should be given.

■ A rounded, positive and myth free picture of the prestigious universities should be presented, and the merits of attending university – of whatever status – should be sold to pupils early on.

A salute

This book has demonstrated that Black boys can make it and how they do so. Their achievement should be celebrated and valorised. But there is no justification for their having to be subjected to the testing challenges reported here or make enormous personal sacrifices simply to get to university. Such challenges far exceed what any child in affluent countries like Britain and America should be expected to overcome. How many people, of whatever class, gender or race, could push through such barriers and get to the finishing line? On behalf of everyone involved in the Black Boys Can network, I salute Black boys who have pushed forth the boundaries and achieved academic success.

Appendix

Interview Schedule

Personal Data

1. Name

2. Age

3. How do you describe yourself in terms of ethnicity?

Success factors

1. Do you see yourself as been educationally successful to date? If so why, if not why not?

2. To what or whom do you attribute your educational success to date?

3. Who were your role models during your schooling years?

Family

1. Did you live in a single or two parent household for most of your school years?

2. Did you grow up with siblings? If so, how many?

3. Have any of your older siblings been to university?

4. Have any of your relatives been to university?

5. What is the highest educational qualifications your parents have obtained?

6. What are your parents' occupations?

7. Did your parents influence on your education? If so, how?

8. What was your school's attitude towards your parents?

9. What was your parents' attitude towards your teachers?

10. What social class do you feel you belong to?

11. What type of neighbourhood did you grow up in?

School

1. What were the educational standards of the schools in your neighbourhood?

2. What school did you go to and why?

3. What type of school did you attend?

4. What was the ethnic composition?

5. Did you experience racism at school?

6. Have you ever been excluded? If so, how often and for what reasons?

7. Did the curriculum reflect Black culture in any way?

8. Were you ever taught by a Black teacher, and if so what were your views about them?

9. Did you feel best about yourself when you were at home at school or elsewhere?

10. What was your attitude to education and school?

11. What was the attitude of children in your class towards high academic attainment, was it OK to get good grades?

12. If someone were to change the colour of your skin along with any other natural features which distinguish Black people, would anyone know you are Black? If so, how?

Access

1. What degree are you studying?

2. What qualifications and grades did you start University with?

3. Did you get any advice or guidance on selecting a university?

4. What influenced your decision to pursue higher education?

5. What criteria did you employ when selecting a university?

6. Did you consider the subject or the actual course when selecting your degree?

7. How are you financed?

8. Which universities did you apply to and why?

9. What have been your experiences of university as a black male to date?

10. Do you think that Black males face barriers in the employment market? If so, how has that knowledge affected you?

Bibliography

Abraham, A. and Jacobs, W. (1990) *Black and White Students' Perceptions of their College Campuses.* Atlanta: Southern Regional Education Board

Acland, T. and Azmi, W. (1998) 'Expectation and Reality: Ethnic Minorities in Higher Education' in Modood, T. and Acland, T. (eds) (1998) *Race and Higher Education.* London: Policy Studies Institute

Allen, A. (1998) 'What are Ethnic Minorities Looking For'? in Madood, T. and Acland, T. (eds) *Race and Higher Education.* London: Policy Studies Institute

Allen, J. (1999) *Actively Seeking Inclusion.* London: Falmer

Allen, W. R. (1987) Black Colleges Vs White Colleges: The Fork in the Road for Black Students. *Change,* 19, pp28-34

Allmendinger, J. (1989) Educational Systems and Labour Market Outcomes. *European Sociological Review* 5, pp231-250

Anderson, E. (1994) The Code of the Streets. *Atlantic Monthly,* 5, pp81-94

Archer, L. (2003) *Race, Masculinity and Schooling: Muslim Boys and Education.* Berkshire: Open University Press

Ball, S. J. (1991) Power, Conflict, Micro-Politics and All That! in Walford, G. (ed) *Doing Educational Research.* London: Routledge

Ball, S. J., Demo, D. H. and Wedman, J. F. (1998) Family Involvement with Children's Homework: An Intervention in the Middle Grades. *Family Relations,* 47, pp149-57

Barnard, N. (1999) One in Ten Trainees has Racist Attitudes. *Times Educational Supplement,* 16 April

Beresford, E. and Hardie, A. (1996) 'Parents and Secondary Schools: A Different Approach?' in Bastiani, J. and Wolfendale, S. (eds) *Home-School Work in Britain: Review, Reflection and Development.* London: David Fulton

Berndt, T. (1996) 'Transitions in Friendship and Friends' Influence' in Graber, J., Brookes-Gunn, J., and Peterson, A. (eds) *Transitions through Adolescent: International Domains and Contexts.* Mahwah, NJ: Erlbaum

Berting, J., Greyer, F. and Jurkovich, R. (1979) *Problems in International Comparative Research in the Social Science.* Oxford: Pergamon

Black, S. (1996) The Truth about Homework. *American School Board Journal,* 183 (10) pp48-51

Blair, M. (2002) Effective School Leadership: the Multi-Ethnic Context. *British Journal of Sociology of Education,* 23 (2) pp179-191

Blair, M. and Bourne, J. with Coffin, C., Cresse, A. and Kenner, C. (1998) *Making a Difference: Teaching and Learning Strategies in Successful Multi-Ethnic Schools.* London: DfEE

Bleach, K. (1998) What Difference Does it Make? in Bleach, K. *Raising Boys' Achievement in Schools.* Stoke on Trent: Trentham Books

Bleach, K. (2000) *Raising Boys', Achievement in Schools.* Stoke on Trent: Trentham Books

Bourdieu, P. (1984) *Distinction: A Social Critique of the Judgement of Taste.* Cambridge, MA: Harvard University Press

Bourdieu, P. (1986) The Three Forms of Capital in Richardson, J. G. (ed) *Handbook of Theory and Research for the Sociology of Education.* New York: Greenwood Press

Bourdieu, P. and Passeron, J. (1973) Cultural Reproduction and Social Reproduction in Brown, R. (ed) *Knowledge, Education and Cultural Change.* London: Tavistock

Bowles, S. and Gintis, H. (1976) *Schooling in Capitalist America: Educational Reform and the Contradictions of Economic Life.* New York: Basic Books

British Education Research Association (1992) *Ethical Guidelines for Educational Research.* British Education Research Association

Brown, D. and Gary, L. (1991) Religious Socialisation and Educational Attainment among African Americans: An Empirical Assessment. *Journal of Negro Education,* 60 (3) pp411-426

Burchard, E.G., Ziv, E., Coyle, N., Gomez, S. L., Tang, H., Karter, A. J., Mountain, J. L., Perez-Stable, E. J., Sheppar, D. and Risch, N. (2003) The Importance of Race and Ethnic Background in Biomedical Research and Clinical Practice. *New England Journal of Medicine,* 348, pp1170-5

Byfield, C. (2007) The Impact of Religion on the Educational Achievement of Black Boys. *British Journal of Sociology of Education,* 29 (2) pp189-199

Callender, C. (1997) *Education for Empowerment.* Stoke on Trent: Trentham Books

Calley, M. J. (1965) *God's People – West Indian Pentecostalism Sects in England.* Oxford: Oxford University Press

Canale, J., Dunlap, L., Britt, M. and Donahue, T. (1996) The Relative Importance of Various College Characteristics to Students in Influencing their Choice of College. *College Student Journal,* 30, pp214-216

Carroll, S. and Walford, G. (1997) The Child's Voice in School Choice. *Education Management and Administration,* 25 (2) pp169-180

Carter, P. (2003) Black Cultural Capital, Status Positioning and Schooling: Conflicts for Low-Income African American Youth. *Social Problems,* 50 (1) pp136-155

Cazden, C. (1988) *Classroom Discourse: The Language of Teaching and Learning.* Portsmouth, NH: Heinemann

Channer, Y. (1995) *I am a Promise: The School Achievements of British African Caribbeans.* Stoke on Trent: Trentham Books

Cheatham, H. and Steward, J. (1993) *Black Families.* New Brunswick, NJ: Transaction

Chevannes, M. and Reeves, F. (1987) 'The Black Voluntary School Movement: Definition, Context and Prospects' in Troyna, B. (ed), *Racial Inequality in Education.* NY: Routledge

Clark, R. (1992) *Neighbourhood Effects of Dropping out of School among Teenage Boys.* Working Paper. Washington, DC: Urban Institute

Clark, R. M. (1983) *Family Life and School Achievement: Why Poor Black Children Succeed or Fail.* Chicago: University of Chicago Press

Clark, S. B. and Crawford, S. L. (1992) An Analysis of African American First Year College Student Attitudes and Attrition Rates. *Urban Education,* 27, pp59-79

Clarke, A. and Power, S. (1998) *Could Do Better. School Reports and Parents Evening: A Study of Secondary School Practice.* London: Research and Information on State and Education Trust

Coffey, A. and Attkinson, P. (1996) *Making Sense of Qualitative Data.* California: Sage

Commission for Racial Equality (1985) *Swann: A Response from the Commission for Racial Equality.* London: CRE

Connell, J. and Halpern-Felsher, B. (1997) 'How Neighbourhoods Affect Educational Outcomes in Middle Childhood and Adolescence: Conceptual Issues and an Empirical Example', in Brooks-Gunn, J., Duncan, G. and Aber, J. (eds) *Neighbourhood Poverty: Context and Consequences for Children.* New York: Russell Sage Foundation Press

Connell, R., Ashenden, D. J., Kessler, S. and Dowsett, G. W. (1982) *Making the Difference: Schools, Family and Social Division.* London: Allen and Unwin

Conner, H., Tyers, C., Modood, T. and Hillage, J. (2004) *Why the Difference? A Closer Look at Higher Education Minority Ethnic Students and Graduates.* Research Report no 552: DFES

Cooper, H., Lindsay, J., Nye, B. and Greathouse, S. (1998) Relationships Between Attitudes About Homework, Amount of Homework Assigned and Completed, and Student Achievement. *Journal of Educational Psychology,* 90, pp70-83

Cooper, R. S., Kaufman, J. S., Ward, R. (2003) 'Race and Genomics'. *New England Journal of Medicine,* 348 (12) pp1166-70

Cork, L. (2005) *Supporting Black Pupils and Parents: Understanding and Improving Home-School Relations.* London: Routledge

Corno, L. (1996) Homework is a Complicated Thing. *Educational Researcher,* 25 (8) pp 27-30

Cotton, T. (1998) *Thinking about Teaching.* Abington: BooKpoint

Coulton, C., Korbin, J., Su, M. and Chow, J. (1995) Community Level Factors and Child Maltreatment Rates. *Child Development,* 66, pp1262-1276

Crane, J. (1991) The Epidemic Theory of Ghettos and Neighbourhood Effects on Dropping Out and Teenage Childbearing. *American Journal of Sociology,* 96 (5) pp1226-59

Crozier, G. (2000) *Parents and Schools: Partners or Protagonists?* Stoke on Trent: Trentham Books

Crozier, G. and Reay, D. (2005) *Activating Participation: Parents and Teachers Working Towards Partnership.* Stoke on Trent: Trentham Books

D'Augelli, A. R. and Hershberger, S. L. (1993) African American Undergraduates on a Predominantly White campus: Academic Factors, Social Networks, and Campus Climate. *The Journal of Negro Education,* 62, pp67-81

Davison, A. and Edwards, C. (1998) 'A Different Style of Learning,' in Bleach, K. (ed) *Raising Boys' Achievement in Schools.* Stoke on Trent: Trentham Books

Day, C. (2004) *A Passion for Teaching.* London: Routledge Falmer

Dearing, Sir, Ron (1997) *National Committee of Enquiry in Higher Education.* The Dearing Report: HMSO

De Lima, P. (2001) *Needs not Numbers: Rural Racism in Scotland.* Scotland: Inverness College and Commission for Racial Equality

Department of Education and Science (1985) *Assisted Places at Independent Schools: A Brief Guide for Parents.* London: DES

Department for Education and Skills (2003) *Aiming High: Raising the Achievement of Minority Ethnic Pupils.* London: DfES

Department for Education and Skills (2004) *Aiming High: Understanding the Educational Needs of Minority Ethnic Pupils in Mainly White Schools.* Guidance: Pupil Support: Equal Opportunities, 0416/2004 London: DfES

Department for Education and Skills (2005) Ethnicity and Education: The Evidence on Minority Ethnic Pupils. *Research Topic Paper,* RTP01-05. London: DfES

Desforges, C. and Abouchaar, A. (2003) *The Impact of Parental Involvement, Parental Support and Family Learning on Pupil Achievement and Adjustment: A Literature Review.* Research Report No. 433: DfES

Donald, J. and Rattansi, A. (1992) *Race, Culture and Difference.* London: Sage

Dornbusch, S., Ritter, P. and Steinberg, L. (1991) Community Influences on the Relation of Family Statuses to Adolescent School Performance: Differences between African-American and Non-Hispanic Whites. *American Journal of Education* 99 (4) pp543-67

DuBois, W. E. (1899) *The Philadelphia Negro: A Social Study.* PA: University of Pennsylvania Press

Duncan, G. (1994) Families and Neighbours as Sources of Disadvantage in the Schooling Decisions of White and Black Adolescents. *American Journal of Education,* 103 (1) pp20-53

Edwards, A. and Polite, C. (1992) *Children of the Dream: The Psychology of Black Success.* New York: Doubleday

Edwards, R. and Alldred, P. (1998) Bodily Location in Home-School Relations: Children's Understanding. *Paper presented at the British Sociological Association Annual Conference.* University of Edinburgh, 6-9 April

Ellen, I. and Turner, M. (1997) Does Neighbourhood Matter? Assessing Recent Evidence. *Housing Policy Debate,* 8 (4) pp833-866

Ellison, C. (1992) Are Religious People Nice People? Evidence from the National Survey of Black Americans. *Social Forces,* 71 (2) pp 411-430

Erickson, B. (1996) Culture, Class and Connections. *American Journal of Sociology,* 102, pp217-251

Evans, W., Oates, W. and Schwab, R. (1992) Measuring Peer Group Effects: A Study of Teenage Behaviour. *Journal of Political Economy,* 100 (51) pp966-991

Eysenck, H. J. (1971) *Race, Intelligence and Education.* London: Temple Smith

Farrell, E. (1994) *Self and School Success. Voices and Lore of Inner-City Students.* Albany: State University of New York Press

Feagin, J., Vera, H. and Imani, N. (1996) *The Agony of Education: Black Students at White Colleges and Universities.* New York: Routledge

Feinberg, W. (1998) *On Higher Ground: Education and the Case for Affirmative Action.* New York: Teachers College Press

Flynn, J. R. (1980) *Race, IQ and Jensen.* London: Routledge and Kegan Paul

Ford, D. (1995) *Reversing Underachievement among Gifted Black Students: Promising Practices and Programmes.* New York: Teachers College Press

Fordham, S. and Ogbu, J. (1986) Black Students School Success: Coping with the Burden of 'Acting White'. *The Urban Review,* 18, pp176-206

Foster, M. (1989) It's Cooking Now: A performance analysis of the speech events of a Black Teacher in an Urban Community College. *Language in Society,* 18 (1) pp1-29

Francis, B. (1999) Lads, Lasses and (New) Labour: 14 Year Old Student Responses to the Laddish Behaviour and Boys' Underachievement Debate. *British Journal of Sociology of Education,* 20 pp357-73

Francis, B. (2000) *Boys, Girls and Achievement.* London: Routledge Falmer

Francis, B. and Skelton, C. (2005) *Reassessing Gender and Achievement: Questioning Contemporary Key Debates.* London: Routledge

Frederick D. Patterson Research Institute of the College Fund/UNCF (1999) *Two Decades of Progress: African Americans Moving Forward in Higher Education.* VA: Fairfax

Freeman, K. (1999) The Race Factor in African Americans College Choice. *Urban Education*, 34, pp4-25

Fries-Britt, S. (1998) Moving Beyond Black Achiever Isolation: Experiences of Gifted Black Collegians. *The Journal of Higher Education*, 69 (5) pp556-576

Gaine, C. (1995) Anti-Racist Education in White Areas: The Limits and Possibilities of Change. *Race, Ethnicity and Education*, 3 (1) pp65-81

Galis, L. (1993) Merely Academic Diversity. *The Journal of Higher Education*, 64 (1) pp93-101

Gallup, G. Jr and Castelli, J. (1989) *The People's Religion: American Faith in the 1990's*. New York: MacMillan

Gallup, G. Jr. (1996) *Religion in America 1996*. NJ: Princeton Religion Research Centre

Galster, G. and Killen, S. (1995) The Geography of Metropolitan Opportunity: A Reconnaissance and Conceptual Framework. *Housing Policy Debate*, 6 (1) pp7-43

Garbarino, J., Dubrow, N., Kostelny, K. and Pardo, C. (1992) *Children in Danger: Coping with the Consequences of Community Violence*. San Francisco: Jossey-Bass

Garner, C and Raudenbus, S. (1971) Neighbourhood Effects on Educational Attainment: A Multilevel Analysis. *Sociology of Education*, 64 (4) pp251-262

Gewirtz, S., Ball, S. and Bowe, R. (1995) *Markets, Choice and Equity in Education*. Buckingham: Open University Press

Ghouri, N. (1998) Race Chief Attracts Training Negligence, *Times Educational Supplement*, 3 July

Gibbs, J. T. (1988) *Young, Black and Male in America: An Endangered Species*. New York: Auburn House

Gibson, M. A. and Ogbu, J. U. (1991) *Minority Status and Schooling: A Comprehensive Study of Immigrant and Involuntary Minorities*. New York: Garland Publishing

Giddens, A. (1991) *The Consequences of Modernity*. Cambridge: Polity Press

Giddens, A. (1995) *Politics, Sociology and Social Theory: Encounters with Classical and Contemporary Social Thought*. Cambridge: Polity Press

Gillborn, D. (1990) *Race, Ethnicity and Education: Teaching and Learning in Multi-Ethnic Schools*. London: Routledge

Gillborn, D. (2002) 'Racism, Policy and the (mis) education of Black children' in Majors, R. (ed) *Educating our Black Children: New Directions and Radical Approaches*. London: Routledge Falmer

Gillborn, D. and Gipps, C. (1996) *Recent Research on the Achievement of Ethnic Minority Pupils*. London: Ofsted

Gipps C. (1994) *Beyond Testing: Towards a Theory of Educational Assessment*. London: Falmer Press

Gipps, C. and Murphy, P. (1994) *A Fair Test? Assessment, Achievement and Equity*. Buckingham: Open University Press

Giroux, H. (1994) Insurgent Multiculturalism and the Promise of Pedagogy. In D.T. Goldberg (ed.) *Multiculturalism: A Critical Reader* (pp.325-343)

Glaeser, E., Laibson, D. and Sacerdote, B. (2002) An Economic Approach to Social Capital. *Economic Journal*, 112, pp437-458

Glaeser, E. and Sacerdote, B. (2001) Education and Religion. National Bureau of Economic Research. *Harvard Institute of Economic Research*, Paper no 1913

Goldthorpe, J. (1980) *Social Mobility Class Structure in Modern Britain*. Oxford: Clarendon Press

Goodson, I. (1992) *Studying Teachers Lives*. London: Routledge

Goodson, I. and Sikes, P. (2001) *Life History Research in Educational Setting: Learning from Lives*. Buckingham: Open University Press

Gourdine, A. and Smitherman, G. (1992) *By Any Means Necessary... Towards The Curriculum Of Struggle*. NJ: African World Press

Green, R. (1995) High Achievement, Underachievement, and Learning Disabilities in Ryan, B. A., Adams, B. R., Gullotta, T. P., Weissberg R. P, and Hampton, R. L. (eds) *The Family-School Connection: Theory, Research, Practice*. CA: Sage

Greene, J. and Winters, M. (2006) Leaving Boys Behind: Public High School Graduation Rates. *Civic Report,* no 48 April

Grenfell, M., James, D., Hodkinson, P., Reay, D. and Robbins, D. (1998) *Bourdieu and Education: Acts of Theory and Practice*. London: Falmer Press

Guthrie, J. W. and Bodenhausen, J. (1984) 'The United States of American' in Hough, J. (ed) *Educational Policy, an International Survey.* New York: St. Martin's Press

Hall, J. (1992) 'The Capitals of Culture: A Non-Holistic Approach to Status Situations, Class, Gender and Ethnicity' in Lamont, M. and Fournier, M. (eds) *Cultivating Differences: Symbolic Boundaries and the Making of Equality.* Chicago: University of Chicago Press

Halpern-Felsher, B., Connell, J., Spencer, M., Aber, J., Duncan, G., Clifford, G., Crichlow, W., Usinger, P. and Cole, S. (1997) Neighbourhood and Family Factors Predicting Educational Risk and Attainment in African-American and White Children and Adolescents, in Brooks-Gunn, J., Duncan, G. and Aber, J. (eds) *Neighbourhood Poverty: Context and Consequences for Children*. New York: Russell Sage Foundation Press

Hamilton, C., Rejtman, R. and Roberts, M. (1999) *Racism and Race Relations in Predominantly White Schools: Preparing Pupils for Life in a Multi-Cultural Society.* Essex: Children's Legal Centre

Hammersley, M. (1984) *The Researcher Exposed: A Natural History in Burgess, R. G. (ed) The Research Process in Educational Setting: Ten Case Studies*. London: Falmer

Hammersley, M. and Atkinson, P, (1995) *Ethnography: Principles in Practice.* London: Routledge

Hansen, D. (1999) 'Conceptions of Teaching and their Consequences' in Lang, M., Olson, J., Hansen, H. and Bunder, J. (eds) *Changing Schools/Changing Practices: Perspectives on Educational Reform and Teacher Professionalism*. Louvain: Grarant

Hanson, S, and Gingsburg, A. (1988) Gaining Ground: Values and High School Success. *American Educational Research Journal*, 25 (3) pp334-365

Helsby, G., Knight, P., McCulloch G., Sanders, M. and Warburton, T. (1997) *Professionalism in Crisis: A report to Participants on the Professional Cultures of Teachers Project*. Lancaster University, January 1997

Herrnstein, R. A. and Murray, C. (1994) *The Bell Curve: Intelligence and Class Structure in American Llife*. New York: Grove Press

Hinds, D. (1995) Talking It Over: How to Get the Boys to the Top of the Class. *The Independent*, Section 2. 26/10/95, pp12-13

HM Inspectorate (1985) *Good Teachers*. Education Observed

Hopkins, R. (1997) *Educating Black Males: Critical Lessons in Schooling, Community and Power.* NY: State University of New York Press

Horvat, E. (1996) *African American Students and College Choice Decision Making in Social Context: The Influence of Race and Class on Educational Opportunity*. Los Angeles, CA: Graduate School of Education and Information Studies

Horvat, E. and Lewis, K. (2003) Reassessing the 'Burden of Acting White'. The Importance of Black Peer Groups in Managing Academic Success. *Sociology of Education*, 76 (10) pp.265-280

Hossler, D. and Gallagher, K. (1987) Studying Student College Choice: A Three-Phase Model and the Implications for Policy Makers. *College and University*, 62 (3) pp207-221

Hunt, L. and Hunt, J. (1975) A Religious Factor in Secular Achievement Among Blacks: The Case of Catholicism. *Social Forces*, 53, (4) pp595-605

Huntsinger, C. (1999) Does K-5 Homework Mean Higher Test Scores? *American Teacher,* 83 (7) pp4

Iannaccone, L. (1998) Introduction to the Economics of Religion. *Journal of Economic Literature* 36 (3) pp1465-1495

Irvine, J. (1990) *Black Students and School Polices, Practices and Prescriptions.* NY: Greenwood Press

Jackson, C. (2003) Motives for Laddishness' at Schools: Fear of Failure and Fear of the 'Feminine'. *British Educational Journal*, 24 (4) pp583-98

Jenks, C. and Mayer, S. (1990a) 'Residential Segregation, Job Proximity, and Black Job Opportunities', in Lynn, L. Jr., and McGeary, M. *Inner-City Poverty in the United States.* Washington DC: National Academy Press

Jensen, D. (1969) How Much Can We Boost IQ and Scholarship Achievement? *Harvard Educational Review*, 39 (1) pp1-23

Jeynes, W. (2003) The Effects of Religious Commitment on the Academic Achievement of Urban and Other Children. *Education and Urban Society,* 36 (1) pp44-62

John, G. (1993) *Building on Strengths, Eliminating Weaknesses: A Developmental Perspective. Paper presented to Asian and African Caribbean Teachers.* London Borough of Hackney

Johnson, D. and Ransom, A. (1988) 'Family and School: The Relationship Reassessed' in Bastiani, J. (ed) *Parents and Teachers Part 2.* Slough: NFER-Nelson

Judd, J. (1999) Young, Gifted, Black and a Living Reproach to our Racist School System. *The Independent*, 11th March

Kerckhoff, A. (1977) The Realism of Educational Ambitions in England and the United States. *American Sociological Review*, 42, pp563-571

Kerckhoff, A. (1993) *Diverging Pathways: Social Structure and Career Deflections.* Cambridge: Cambridge University Press

Kerckhoff, A. and Bell, L. (1998) Hidden Capital: Vocational Credentials and Attainment in the United States. *Sociology of Education,* 71, pp152-174

Kerckhoff, A., Hanley, L. and Glennie, E. (2001) System Effects on Educational Achievement: A British-American Comparison. *Social Science Research*, 30 (4) pp479-582

Kinder, K., Wakefield, A. and Wilkin, A. (1996) *Talking Back: Pupils' View on Disaffection.* Slough: NFER-Nelson

Kreisberg, S. (1992) *Transforming Power: Domination, Empowerment and Education.* NY: State University of New York Press

Kvale, S. (1996) *An Introduction to Qualitative Research Interviewing.* London: Sage Publications

Labour Party Press Release, 13 July, 1981, in Walford, G. (1990) *Privatisation and Privilege in Education.* London: Routledge

Ladson-Billings, G. (1990) 'Culturally Relevant Teaching'. *The College Board Review,* 155, pp200-225

Lamont, M. and Lareau, A. (1988) 'Cultural Capital: Allusions, Gaps and Glissandos' in *Recent Theoretical Developments' Sociological Theory*, 6 (153) pp153-168

Lareau, A. (1989) *Home Advantage: School, Class and Parental Intervention in Elementary Education.* New York: Falmer Press

Larson, E. (1985) *Trial and Error: The American Controversy over Creation and Evolution.* Oxford: Oxford University Press

Leitch, R., Mitchell, S. and Kilpatrick, R. (2003) *A Study into Potential Models for the Successful Teaching of Personal Development in the Northern Ireland Curriculum.* Report to the Department of Education

Lewis, P. (2000) An Enquiry into Male Wastage from Primary ITE Courses at a University College and Success Indicators for Retention. Paper presented to Recruitment and Retention of Teachers Seminar Conference at the University of North London, 19 January

Lewis-Rhodes, A. and Nam, C. The Religious Context of Educational Expectations. *American Sociological Review*, 35 (2) pp253-267

Lightfoot, L. (1997) Attention Span of Boys Only Five Minutes. *Daily Telegraph.* 26/4/97

Lightfoot, S. (1973) Politics and Reasoning: Through the Eyes of Teachers and Children. *Harvard Educational Review*, 43 (2) 197-244

Lincoln, C. E. and Mamiya, L. (1990) *The Black Church in the African American Experience.* NC: Duke University Press

Litten, L. (1982) Different Strokes in the Applicant Pool: Some Refinements in a Model of Student Choice. *Journal of Higher Education*, 53 (4) pp383-402

Littlejohn-Blake, S. and Darling, C. (1993) Understanding the Strengths of African American Families. *Journal of Black Studies,* 23 (4) pp460-471

Ludwig, J. (1993) *Information and Inner City Educational Attainment.* Mimeo: Georgetown University

Mac an Ghaill, M. (1988) *Young Gifted and Black: Student-Teacher Relations in the Schooling of Black Youth.* Milton Keynes: Open University Press

Mac an Ghaill, M. (1991) Black Voluntary Schools: The Invisible Private Sector in Walford, G. (ed) *Private Schooling: Tradition, Change and Diversity.* London: Paul Chapman

Mac an Ghaill, M. (1994) *The Making of Men.* Buckingham: Open University Press

Mac an Ghaill, M. (1999 New Cultures of Training: Emerging Male (hetero) Sexual Identities. *British Educational Research Journal*, 25, pp419-25

Majors, R. and Billson, J. (1992) *Cool Pose: The Dilemmas of Black Manhood in America.* New York: Lexington Books

Majors, R. (2001) (ed) *Educating Our Black Children.* London: Routledge Falmer

Marshall, G., Rose, D., Newby, H. and Vogler, C. (1988) *Social Class in Modern Britain.* London: Unwin Hyman

Martin, N. and Dixon, P. (1991) Factors Influencing Students, College Choice. *Journal of College Student Development,* 32, pp253-257

Martinez, P. and Richters, J. (1993) The NIMH Community Violence Project: Children's Distress Symptoms Associated with Violence Exposure. *Psychiatry,* 56 pp22-35

Mascias, J. (1987) The Hidden Curriculum of Papago Teachers: American Indian Strategies for Mitigating Cultural Discontinuity in Early Schooling, in Spindler, G. and Spindler, L. (eds), *Interpretative Ethnography at Home and Abroad.* Hillsdale, NJ: Lawrence Erlbaum Associates

Mason, D. (1986) 'Introduction, Controversies and Continuities in Race and Ethnic Relations Theory' in Rex, J. and Mason (eds) *Theories in Race and Ethnic Relations.* Cambridge: Cambridge University Press

Mason, J. (2002) *Qualitative Researching.* London: Sage

May, S. and Modood, T. (2001) *Ethnicities* 1 (1) pp5-7

Mayer, C. (1996) Does Location Matter? *New England Economic Review*, 5, pp26-40

McAdoo, H. P. (1988) *Black Families.* CA: Sage

McDermott, R. (1984) When School Goes Home: Some Problems in the Organisation of Homework. *Teachers College Record*, 84 (3) pp391-409

Miles, M. and Humerman, A. (1994) *Qualitative Data Analysis*. CA: Sage

Modood, T. (1994) The End of Hegemony: The Concept of Black and British Asians in Rex, J. and Drury, B. (ed) *Ethnic Mobilisation in a Multicultural Europe*. Aldershot: Averbury Press

Modood, T. and Acland, T. (1998) *Race and Higher Education*. London: London Policy Studies Institute

Modood, T. and Shiner, M. (1994) *Ethnic Minorities and Higher Education*. London: London Policy Studies Institute

Morgan, C. and Morris, G. (1999) *Good Teaching and Learning: Pupils and Teachers Speak*. Buckingham: Open University Press

Mortimer, J. and Kriger, H. (2000) Pathways from School to Work in Germany and the United States, in Hallinan, M. (ed.) *Handbook of the Sociology of Education*. New York: Kluwer Academic/ Plenum

Mortimore, P., Sammons, P., Stoll, L., Lewis, D. and Ecob, R. (1988) *School Matters: The Junior Years*. Wells: Open Books

National Commission on Education (1996) *Success against the Odds: Effective Schools in Disadvantaged Areas*. London: Routledge

National Committee of Inquiry into Higher Education (Dearing Report): Report with Evidence/ Select Committee on Science and Technology (1997). Parliament, House of Lords, Select Committee on Science and Technology. London: Stationery Office

NEAB (1996) Gender Differences in the GCSE. *NEAB Standard*, Summer 1996, pp6-7

Nettles, M. and Perna, L. (1997) *The African American Education Data Book*. Fairfax, VA: The Frederick D. Patterson Research Institute of the College Fund/UNCF

Noble, C., Brown, J. and Murphy, J. (2001) *How to Raise Boys' Achievement*. London: David Fulton Publishers

Ofsted (1999) *Raising the Attainment of Minority Ethnic Pupils: Schools and LEA's Response*. London: Ofsted

Ofsted/EOC (1996) *The Gender Divide*. London: HMSO

Ogbu J. U. (1988) Class stratification, Racial Stratification and Schooling in Weis, L. (ed) *Class and Gender in American Education*. Albany: State University of New York Press

Ogbu J. U. (1992) Understanding Cultural Diversity and Learning. *Educational Researcher*, 21, pp5-14

Ogbu, J. U. (1998) Voluntary and Involuntary Minorities: A Cultural Ecological Theory of School Performance with some Implications for Education. *Anthropology and Education*, 29 (2) pp155-188

O'Leary, J. and Betts, H. (1999) Inspectors Accuse Schools of Racism. *The Times*, 11 March

Osborne, J. W. (1997) Race and Academic Disidentification. *Journal of Educational Psychology*, 89, pp728-735

Osborne, J. W. (2001) 'Testing Stereotype Threat: Does Anxiety Explain Race and Sex Differences in Achievement?' *Contemporary Educational Psychology*, 26, pp291-310

Osler, A. (1997) *The Education and Careers of Black Teachers*. Buckingham: Open University Press

Pattilio-McCoy, M. (1998) Church Culture as a Strategy of Action in the Black Community. *American Sociological Review*, 63 (6) pp767-784

Paulsen, M. (1990) College Choice: Understanding Student Enrolment Behaviour *Report No. EDO-HE-60-90*. Washington, DC: ERIC Clearing House on Higher Education

Person, D. and Christensen, M. (1996) Understanding Black Student Culture and Black Student Retention. *NASPA*, 34, pp47-56

Ploch, D. and Hastings, D. (1994) Graphic Presentations of Church Attendance Using General Social Survey Data. *Journal for the Scientific Stay of Religion*, 33, pp16-33

Plotnick, R. and Hoffman, S. (1996) The Effect of Neighbourhood Characteristics on Young Adult Outcomes, in *IRP Discussion Paper* No. 1106-96. Madison, WI: Institute for Research on Poverty

Pollard, D. (1989) Against the Odds: A Profile of Academic Achievers from the Urban Underclass. *The Journal of Negro Education*, 58 (3) pp297-308

Preece, J. (1999) Families into Higher Education Project: An Awareness Raising Action Research Project with Schools and Parents. *Higher Education Quarterly*, 53 (3) pp197-210

Price, J. N. (2000) *Against the Odds*. Greenwich: Ablex Publishing Company

Punch, K. (1998) I*ntroduction to Social Research: Qualitative and Qualitative Approaches.* London: Sage

Putnam, R. (2000) *Bowling Alone: The Collapse and Revival of American Community.* New York: Simon and Schuster

Rampton, (1981) *West Indian Children in Our Schools.* London: HMSO

Reay, D. (2002a) A Useful Extension of Bourdieu's Conceptual Framework? Emotional Capital as a Way of Understanding Mothers Involvement in Children's Schooling'. *Sociological Review*, 48 (4) pp568-585

Reay, D., Davies, J., David, M. and Ball, S. (2001) Choices of Degree and Degrees of Choice. *Sociology,* 35, pp855-874

Reay, D. and Luey, H. (2002) I Don't Like it Here, But I Don't Want to be Anywhere Else: Children Living on Inner City London Council Estates. *Antipode,* 32 (4) pp410-28

Regnerus, M. (2000) Shaping Schooling Success: Religious Socialisation and Educational Outcomes in Metropolitan Public Schools. *Journal for the Scientific Study of Religion*, 39 (3) pp363-370

Reinharz, S. (1992) *Feminist Methods in Social Research*. Oxford: Oxford University Press

Rhamie, J. (2007) *Eagles Who Soar: how Black learners find the path to success*. Stoke on Trent: Trentham

Rhamie, J. and Hallam, S. (2002) An Investigation into African Caribbean Academic Success in the UK. *Race, Ethnicity and Education,* 5, (2) pp151-168

Ricketts, E. and Sawhill, I. (1998) Defining and Measuring the Underclass. *Journal of Policy Analysis and Management,* 7, pp316-25

Roberts, K. (1980) 'Schools, Parents and Social Class' in Craft, M., Raynor, J. and Cohen, L. (eds) *Linking School and Home.* London: Harper and Row

Robson, C. (1993) *Real World Research*. Oxford: Blackwell

Rosenberg, N. A., Pritchard, J.K., and Weber, J.L., (2002) 'Genetic Structure of Human Populations. *Science*, 298 pp2381-5

Ross, M. J. (1998) *Success Factors of Young African American Males at a Historically Black College*. Connecticut: Bergin and Garvey

Salisbury, J. and Jackson, D. (1996) *Challenging Macho Values*. London: Falmer

Salter, B. and Tapper, T. (1985) *Power and Policy in Education: The Case of Independent Schooling.* East Sussex: Falmer Press

Sammons, P. (1995) Gender, Ethnic and Socio-Economic Differences in Attainment and Progress: A Longitudinal Analysis of Student Achievement over 9 Years. *British Educational Research Journal*, 21 (4) p465-85

Schloredt, V. and Brown, P. (1988) *Martin Luther King.* Watford: Exley

Sevier, R. (1992) Recruiting African American Undergraduates: A National Survey of the Factors that Affect Institutional Choice. *College and University,* 68, pp48-51

Sewell, T. (1997) *Black Masculinity and Schooling: How Black Boys Survive Modern Schooling.* Stoke on Trent: Trentham Books

Shuker, N. (1988) *Martin Luther King.* London: Burke

Sibbitt, R. (1997) *The Perpetrators of Racist Violence and Harassment.* London: Home Office

Skelton, C. (2001a) *Schooling the Boys.* Buckingham: Open University Press

Slater, R. B. (1994) The Growing Gap in Black Higher Education. *The Journal of Blacks in Higher Education,* 3, pp52-59

Smith, D. and Tomlinson, S. (1989) *The School Effect: A Study of Multi-Racial Comprehensives.* London: Policy Studies Institute

Smith, V. (1997) 'Caring: Motivation for African American Male Youths to Succeed'. *Journal of African American Men,* 3 (2) pp49-63

Smithers, A. (1996) New Myths of the Gender Gap. *Times Educational supplement,* 3/5/96, pp18

Sockett, H. (1993) *The Moral Base for Teacher Professionalism.* Columbia University: Teachers College Press

Soderman, A. and Phillips, M (1986) The Early Education of Males: Where Are We Failing Them? *Educational Leadership,* 44, (3) pp70-72

Spencer, M. (1991) Adolescent African American Self Esteem: Suggestions for Mentoring Program Content. *Conference Paper Series.* Washington: Urban Institute

Spencer, M., Brookins, G. and Allen, W. (1985) *Beginnings: The Social and Affective Development of Black Children.* Hillside, NJ: Lawrence Erlbaum.

Stark, R., Iannaccone, L. and Finke, R. (1996) Religion, Science and Rationality. *American Economic Review,* 86 (2) pp433-37

Steel, C., and Aronson, J. (1995) Stereotype Threat and the Intellectual Test Performance of African-Americans. *Journal of Personality and Social Psychology,* 69 (5) pp797-811

Steinberg, L. and Silverberg, S. (1986) The Vicissitudes of Autonomy in Early Adolescence. *Child Development,* 57, pp841-51

Swann, M. (1985) *Education for All: Final Report of the Committee of Inquiry into the Education of Children from Ethnic Minority Groups.* Cmnd 9453, London: HMSO

Swartz, D. (1997) *Culture and Power: The Sociology of Pierre Bourdieu.* Chicago: University of Chicago Press

Taylor, P. (1992) Ethnic Group Data and Applications to Higher Education. *Higher Education Quarterly,* 4614, pp359-374

Taylor, R., Chatters, R. and Levin, J. (1996) Black and White Differences in Religious Participation: A Multisample Comparison. *Journal for the Scientific Study of Religion,* 35 (4) pp403-410

Tesch, R. (1990) *Qualitative Research – Analysis Types and Software Tools.* New York: Falmer Press

Tizzard, B., Blatchford, P., Burke, J., Farquhar, C. and Plewis, I. (1988) *Young Children at School in the Inner City.* Hove: Lawrence Erlbaum Associates

Tomlinson, S. (1977) Race and Education in Britain 1960-77: An Overview of the Literature. *Sage Race Relations Abstracts,* 2 (4) pp3-33

Tomlinson, S. (1983a) *Ethnic Minorities in British Schools: A Review of Literature 1960-1982.* London: Heinemann

Tomlinson, S. (1983b) 'Black Women in Higher Education – Case Studies of University Women in Britain', in Barton, L. and Walker, S. (eds) *Race, Class and Education*. London: Croom Helm

Tomlinson, S. (1991) Home School Partnerships. *Education and Training*. Paper No 7, London: Institute for Public Policy Research

Tomlinson, S. (1992) Disadvantaging the Disadvantaged: Bangladeshi's and Education in Tower Hamlets. *British Journal of Sociological Education*, 13 (4) pp437-46

Tooley, J. and Derby, D. (1998) *Educational Research: An Ofsted Critique*. London: Ofsted

Troyna, B. and Hatcher, R. (1992) *Racism in Children's Lives: A Study of Mainly White Schools*. London: Routledge

US Census Bureau, Population Division, Education and Social Stratification Branch. Revised June 2004

US Department of Education (1995) *Child Care and Early Education Program Participation of Infants, Toddlers, and Preschoolers*. National Centre for Education, Washington DC: Statistics Publication No. 95824

Vincent, C. (1996) *Parents and Teachers: Power and Participation*. London: Falmer Press

Vispoel, W. and Astin, J. (1995) Success and Failure in Junior High School: A Critical Incident Approach to Understanding Studnets Attributional Beliefs. *American Educational Research Journal*, 32 (2) pp377-412

Walford, G. (1990) *Privatisation and Privilege in Education*. London: Routledge

Walford, G. (1994) *Choice and Equity in Education*. London: Cassell

Walter, P., Vispoel, W., James, R. and Austin, J. (1995) Success and Failure in Junior High School: A Critical Incident Approach to Understanding Students' Attribution Beliefs. *American Educational Research Journal*, 32 (2) pp377-412

Watt, D., Sheriffe, G. and Majors, R. (1999) Mentoring Black Male Pupils. Unpublished manuscript: City College Manchester

Weis, L. (1988) *Class, Race and Gender in American Education*. New York: State University of New York Press

White, R. (2000) *The School of Tomorrow: Values and Vision*. Buckingham: Open University Press

Whitty, G., Power, S. and Halpin, D. (1998) *Devolution and Choice in Education: The School, The State, and The Market*. Maidenhead: Open University Press

Willis, P. (1977) *Learning to Labour*. Farnborough: Saxon House

Wilson, J. (1987) T*he Truly Disadvantaged: The Inner City, the Underclass, and Public Policy*. Chicago: University of Chicago Press.

Wilson, W. (1991) Studying Inner-City Dislocations: The Challenge for Public Agenda Research: 1990 Presidential Address. *American Sociological Review*, 56, pp56:1-14

Wilson-Sadberry, K., Winfield, L. and Royster, D. (1991) Resilience and Persistence of African American Males in Postsecondary Enrolment. *Education and Urban Society*, 24 (1) pp87-102

Woods, P. and Jeffrey, B (1996) *Teachable Moments: The Art of Teaching in Primary Schools*. Buckingham: Open University Press

Wright, E. (1980) *Class and Occupation. Theory and Society*, 9, pp177-214

Yin, R. (1999) *Case Study Research: Design and Methods*. Thousand Oaks: Sage Publications

Younger, M., Warrington, M. and McLellan, R. (2005) *Raising Boys' Achievements in Secondary Schools: Issues, Dilemmas and Opportunities*. Maidenhead: Open University Press

Index